EDITIONS

ARMENIAN
BULGARIAN
BURMESE (Myanmar)
CHINESE
DUTCH
ENGLISH
  Africa
  Australia
  Chinese/English
  India
  Indonesia
  Indonesian/English
  Japan
  Korean/English
  Korean/English/
    Japanese
  Myanmar
  Philippines
  Singapore
  Sri Lanka
  United Kingdom
  United States
ESTONIAN
FRENCH
GREEK
GUJARATI
HINDI
HUNGARIAN
IBAN/ENGLISH
ILOKANO
INDONESIAN
ITALIAN
JAPANESE
KANNADA
KOREAN
MALAYALAM
NEPALI
NORWEGIAN
ODIA
POLISH
PORTUGUESE
  Africa
  Brazil
  Portugal
RUSSIAN
SINHALA
SPANISH
  Caribbean
  Mexico
  South America
  United States
SWEDISH
TAMIL
TELUGU
THAI
URDU

THE UPPER ROOM

WHERE THE WORLD MEETS TO PRAY

Susan Hibbins
UK Editor

INTERDENOMINATIONAL
INTERNATIONAL
INTERRACIAL

33 LANGUAGES
Multiple formats are available in some languages

The Bible Reading Fellowship
15 The Chambers, Vineyard
Abingdon OX14 3FE
brf.org.uk

The Bible Reading Fellowship (BRF) is a Registered Charity (233280)

ISBN 978 0 85746 607 5

Originally published in the USA by The Upper Room®
US edition © The Upper Room®
This edition © The Bible Reading Fellowship 2018
Cover image © Thinkstock

Acknowledgements
Scripture quotations marked NRSV are taken from The New Revised Standard Version of the Bible, Anglicised Edition, copyright © 1989, 1995 by the Division of Christian Education of the National Council of the Churches of Christ in the USA. Used by permission. All rights reserved.

Scripture quotations marked NIV are taken from The Holy Bible, New International Version (Anglicised edition) copyright © 1979, 1984, 2011 by Biblica. Used by permission of Hodder & Stoughton Publishers, an Hachette UK company. All rights reserved. 'NIV' is a registered trademark of Biblica. UK trademark number 1448790.

Extracts marked KJV are from the Authorised Version of the Bible (The King James Bible), the rights in which are vested in the Crown, are reproduced by permission of the Crown's Patentee, Cambridge University Press.

Extracts from CEB copyright © 2011 by Common English Bible.

Map on page 6 © Thinkstock.

Printed by Gutenberg Press, Tarxien, Malta

How to use *The Upper Room*

The Upper Room is ideal in helping us spend a quiet time with God each day. Each daily entry is based on a passage of scripture, and is followed by a meditation and prayer. Each person who contributes a meditation to the magazine seeks to relate their experience of God in a way that will help those who use *The Upper Room* every day.

Here are some guidelines to help you make best use of *The Upper Room*:

1   Read the passage of scripture. It is a good idea to read it more than once, in order to have a fuller understanding of what it is about and what you can learn from it.
2   Read the meditation. How does it relate to your own experience? Can you identify with what the writer has outlined from their own experience or understanding?
3   Pray the written prayer. Think about how you can use it to relate to people you know, or situations that need your prayers today.
4   Think about the contributor who has written the meditation. Some *Upper Room* users include this person in their prayers for the day.
5   Meditate on the 'Thought for the day' and the 'Prayer focus', perhaps using them again as the focus for prayer or direction for action.

Why is it important to have a daily quiet time? Many people will agree that it is the best way of keeping in touch every day with the God who sustains us, and who sends us out to do his will and show his love to the people we encounter each day. Meeting with God in this way reassures us of his presence with us, helps us to discern his will for us and makes us part of his worldwide family of Christian people through our prayers.

I hope that you will be encouraged as you use the magazine regularly as part of your daily devotions, and that God will richly bless you as you read his word and seek to learn more about him.

Susan Hibbins
UK Editor

In times of/For help with . . .

Below is a list of entries in this copy of *The Upper Room* relating to situations or emotions with which we may need help:

Advent/Christmas: Dec 2, 5, 9, 23, 24, 25

Assurance: Sep 23; Oct 2, 5, 6; Nov 22, 25

Bible reading: Sep 7; Oct 23; Dec 30

Change: Sep 12, 28; Oct 9

Christian community: Sep 4, 8; Oct 10, 30; Nov 2; Dec 11, 31

Compassion: Sep 1, 5, 27

Creation/nature's beauty: Oct 2, 14; Nov 27; Dec 4, 30

Death/grief: Sep 23; Oct 25; Dec 6, 17

Doubt: Sep 10, 22; Oct 25

Encouragement: Sep 18; Oct 11; Nov 10, 21; Dec 18, 26

Family: Sep 1, 24; Oct 15, 18, 25; Nov 2, 29; Dec 2, 29

Fear: Sep 17, 29; Nov 3, 6, 21; Dec 3, 21

Forgiveness: Nov 4, 18; Dec 29

Friendship: Sep 11, 19; Oct 8

Generosity/giving: Sep 1, 5; Oct 15; Nov 8; Dec 5, 10

God's goodness/love: Sep 11; Oct 2, 8, 18; Nov 12; Dec 20, 25, 27

God's presence: Sep 4, 29; Oct 5, 29; Nov 6, 15, 27; Dec 6, 17, 24

God's provision: Sep 2, 14, 28; Oct 4; Nov 2, 29; Dec 3, 5, 28

Gratitude: Sep 9; Oct 6; Nov 13, 21, 30

Growth: Sep 14; Oct 3, 30; Nov 21, 29; Dec 1, 21

Guidance: Sep 2; Oct 7, 9, 23; Nov 15; Dec 8, 15, 23

Healing/illness: Sep 17, 29; Oct 5, 14, 16; Nov 3, 9, 24; Dec 24

Hope: Sep 20; Oct 1, 11, 27; Nov 4; Dec 3, 7, 24

Hospitality: Sep 13; Oct 17, 27; Dec 10, 22

Job issues: Sep 3, 9, 12; Nov 5

Judging: Oct 6; Nov 12; Dec 12, 26, 29

Living our faith: Sep 5, 25; Oct 10, 28; Nov 1, 30; Dec 11, 13, 28

Mission/outreach: Sep 5, 30; Oct 13, 30; Nov 7, 11, 28; Dec 22

New beginnings: Sep 19, 28; Oct 16; Nov 5, 23; Dec 31

Obedience: Oct 7, 13; Dec 13

Parenting: Sep 16, 26; Dec 12

Prayer: Sep 3, 10, 26; Oct 1, 4, 20; Nov 26, 28; Dec 8

Renewal: Sep 8, 15; Oct 1, 14, 19, 31; Nov 17

Salvation: Oct 24; Nov 25; Dec 1, 27

Serving: Sep 21, 30; Oct 17, 30; Nov 7, 11; Dec 10

Social issues: Sep 1, 18, 30; Oct 27; Dec 10

Speaking about faith: Oct 22; Nov 13, 28; Dec 9, 13, 31

Spiritual gifts: Sep 21; Oct 13, 26; Nov 10, 29

Spiritual practices: Sep 7, 9, 16, 26; Oct 3, 31; Nov 14, 19; Dec 19

Strength: Sep 17; Oct 3; Nov 9, 17

Stress: Sep 10, 15; Dec 19

Suffering: Oct 19, 25

Tragedy: Sep 15; Oct 25

Trust: Sep 3, 6, 10, 22; Oct 4, 29 Nov 3; Dec 15, 18

Worry: Sep 6; Oct 2

We are called

Each of you should use whatever gift you have received to serve others, as faithful stewards of God's grace in its various forms. (1 Peter 4:10, NIV)

In my church tradition, we pray a prayer of confession during worship each week as a way of acknowledging our humanity and reconciling with God. One version of that prayer begins, 'Merciful God, we confess that we have sinned against you in thought, word, and deed, by what we have done, and by what we have left undone.'

When I pray that prayer, the words 'what we have left undone' weigh most heavily on me. While I certainly act in ways that are hurtful to others, I can usually name those specifically and work to make amends. But things I 'have left undone' could be anything. Perhaps I put my personal spiritual practice off for a less-busy week or ignored someone in need because the thought of interacting with a stranger made me uncomfortable. Or perhaps I have left undone some act of compassion of which I wasn't even aware.

It is significant that we pray this prayer as a congregation. As the scripture verse quoted above reminds us, each of us has been given different spiritual gifts, and each of us is called to serve in various ways. God does not call any one individual to do everything. Instead, God calls us as the body of Christ to use our particular gifts to share his grace with the world; together, we can accomplish all that he has set before us.

In this issue of *The Upper Room*, several writers share their personal experiences of doing and leaving undone and reflect on how they use the spiritual gifts God has given them. As you read, I invite you to consider how God is calling you to use your spiritual gifts to serve others. How will you answer the call?

Lindsay L. Gray
Editorial Director, The Upper Room

Where the world meets to pray

Editions of *The Upper Room* daily devotional guide are printed in:
- Hong Kong (Chinese, Chinese/English)
- Japan (Japanese, English)
- Korea (Korean, Korean/English, and Korean/English/Japanese)

Hong Kong
The Methodist Church, Hong Kong is seeking to expand its outreach and distribution of *The Upper Room* to those employed as domestic workers.

Japan
Copies of each issue of the devotional guide are shared with students at Aoyama Gakuin University in Tokyo.

Korea
Military personnel receive copies of *The Upper Room* through the missionary work of The Korea Christian Leader's Mission.

The Editor writes...

In 2017 I had two knee replacement operations as a result of arthritis. It was a huge relief to have pain-free knees and to be able to walk easily again, but some weeks after the second operation I noticed that my new joint made a clunking sound when I walked. Though this is common, I mentioned it to the physiotherapist, who asked me to walk the length of the gym so that she could watch. Afterwards she said: 'You are walking as if you still have painful knees. You have become so used to compensating for the pain that you are still doing so; you need to learn to walk properly again.' When I corrected my posture and changed the way I walked, the clunking noise disappeared.

Does this remind you of our spiritual lives? It is certainly like mine! We take our concerns to God, our worries and anxieties, planning to leave them all with him, but still we find it hard not to carry them away again. We ask his forgiveness for our anger or resentment or harsh words, and feel ourselves forgiven, yet we still hang on to our hurt feelings or our guilt. Sometimes we think back to previous years of our lives, to earlier decisions which we regret. If only we had our time over again, we say, we would do things very differently.

Regret, resentment, unresolved guilt, looking back... all these things can affect our walk with God, holding us back from the new life which he longs to give us. We are so used to living with such feelings that they have become a part of us. Unconsciously, we are walking in the wrong way. In Isaiah 43:18–19 we read: 'Forget the former things; do not dwell on the past. See, I am doing a new thing! Now it springs up; do you not perceive it?' (NIV). God wants us to move forward in him, free from old hurts that have caused us pain.

When I walk now, I remind myself to put my head up, square my shoulders properly and walk straight, and I am unencumbered by pain. May God grant that we can do the same as we walk in his way.

Susan Hibbins
UK Editor

P.S. I am delighted to include in this issue the meditations by the winner, Sue Richards, and two runners-up, David Butterfield and Edna Hutchings, from BRF's *Upper Room* writing competition. You can read them on 27 September, 12 October and 21 October.

The Bible readings are selected with great care, and we urge you to include the suggested reading in your devotional time.

A child of God

Read Matthew 15:29–39

Do not neglect to show hospitality to strangers, for by doing that some have entertained angels without knowing it.

Hebrews 13:2 (NRSV)

On my way to work, I sometimes saw a homeless man sitting in a wheelchair on the corner, but I always passed him by. Sometimes I would say, 'Good morning', but I couldn't bring myself to ask, 'How are you?' I even wondered whether his wheelchair was necessary or just a prop.

Then one cold, rainy night, my teenage son, Chad, asked me for a flask of hot chocolate. He then asked if he could take an extra blanket. 'Of course,' I said. He pulled the blanket from the cupboard, picked up his hot chocolate, said, 'Thanks Mum,' and went out.

The next morning I trudged off down the street to work. On the corner sat the homeless man. But now his lap was covered with the blanket Chad had taken out the night before. On the pavement near him was the flask that had contained hot chocolate. I thought about how I would do anything for my children, yet I had ignored the needs of this child of God.

I vowed to bring the man lunch the next day, but when I got to the corner, he had gone. I had missed the opportunity to show the compassion that my son had so freely displayed.

Prayer: *Dear God, fill us with compassion so that we will act to help those in need. Amen*

Thought for the day: Today I will see the strangers I meet as children of God.

Vicki Easterly (Kentucky, US)

The winds of life

Read Isaiah 49:8–10

I will instruct you and teach you the way you should go; I will counsel you with my eye upon you.
Psalm 32:8 (NRSV)

I help to run a children's summer camp in Wisconsin, where my daughter Emily taught sailing for a couple of years. One day I went to the lake to watch her sail with the children. When I arrived, Emily's boat was about two miles south of the beach where I sat. I watched my daughter guide the boat against the wind from one side of the lake to the other until she landed her boat close to where I was sitting.

Watching Emily sail that day helped me see how living can be similar to sailing a boat. In life we cannot control the winds of life that blow against us, but we can adjust our response to difficult situations, just as sailors adjust their sails and rudder to arrive at their destination. Fortunately, as Christians, we have a navigator, the Holy Spirit, who is always there to guide us.

Emily's voyage that day was not long. But when sailing across large bodies of water, sailors use navigational charts to show them where they should sail and what they need to be looking out for. Our navigational chart is the Bible. As we grow in wisdom through scripture we become better sailors who can navigate through all the winds of life that blow our way.

Prayer: *Heavenly Father, thank you for your Holy Spirit, our guide who helps us to navigate our lives. Amen*

Thought for the day: The Holy Spirit helps me to find my way against the winds of life.

Rick Jones (Indiana, US)

Perfect peace

Read 1 Thessalonians 5:16–18

I know the plans I have in mind for you, declares the Lord; they are plans for peace, not disaster, to give you a future filled with hope.
Jeremiah 29:11 (CEB)

Arriving home, I slung my briefcase at the sofa. My boss had just informed me that he was about to make me redundant. The school board would meet in one week to decide the fate of the special programme for children that I had spent eight years building. I had lobbied hard for my job and the programme, but the budget was too tight. My boss had decided that the money would be better spent elsewhere. Next year, I would not have a job.

As I tossed and turned that night, I remembered a meditation I had read years earlier, which recommended submitting everything to God's will. Did I have the courage to pray that prayer now? Was I ready to let go of worries about my future and trust God? I struggled with those questions for the next several days as negotiations continued. By Friday evening, after another discouraging day, I was ready. 'Your will be done,' I prayed. 'Lord, I accept whatever you want for my future.' I had not expected to feel such an immediate sense of peace.

When the board met the following Monday, they voted to keep my programme and expand it. This was wonderful. But more wonderful was what I had learned: whatever happens, I can find peace by leaning on God.

Prayer: *Heavenly Father, when our future is uncertain, help us to follow your Son's example – showing us the way to perfect peace when he prayed, 'Not my will, but yours be done' (Luke 22:42, NIV). Amen*

Thought for the day: When I yield my life to God, peace follows.

Ginny Neil (Virginia, US)

Encircling love

Read 1 John 4:7–12

Know that the Lord is God. It is he who made us, and we are his; we are his people, the sheep of his pasture.
Psalm 100:3 (NIV)

Nestled in a hollow on the moor, it was the finest sheepfold I had ever seen. One enormous circle, built of stone from the rocky debris nearby, it provided protection from cold winter winds and snow – a place for the sheep to huddle together for warmth where the shepherd could find them and feed them.

'Why didn't they build it square?' my young companion asked. I pondered a moment before answering. 'It makes the fold more resistant to the wind,' I said. With time to reflect, I came up with more ideas. In a square fold some sheep would end up in the corners – and corners can be cold. The whole purpose of a sheepfold is to be an enfolding embrace – a wrap-around of warmth and security.

Such is the presence of our loving God. Such is the fellowship of his people, the church. No corners! All are held together safe and secure in God's love, ready to move to new pastures when they hear and obediently follow his voice. Square may look smart, but the round encircling love of God proves best.

Prayer: *Dear Lord Jesus, remind us to guard against cold corners in our Christian fellowship. Amen*

Thought for the day: I am always warmed by God's surrounding love.

Colin Harbach (Cumbria, England)

Uncommon kindness

Read Acts 28:1–10
The islanders showed us unusual kindness.
Acts 28:2 (NIV)

In today's scripture reading, Paul was sailing through stormy seas with a large group of people who were scared and beginning to lose hope on their journey to Rome. As they came upon an island, the inhabitants – who had no reason to trust this large group of strangers – showed them uncommon kindness. They built a fire and welcomed their visitors with open arms as fellow humans in need of warmth and sustenance. Paul then showered the islanders with kindness of his own, by using the power of the Holy Spirit to heal every man, woman and child suffering with illness.

How different would this scenario have been if the islanders had turned away the members of Paul's ship out of fear? The kindness continued, as the islanders honoured Paul and the others by giving them all the supplies they would need to continue their journey safely.

How many times have we allowed selfishness, fear or lack of trust to prevent us from behaving similarly to others? What if, instead, we as Christians were to show kindness so uncommon that it surprises the receivers and causes them to wonder where this type of hospitality comes from? In showing such kindness, we would display the love of Christ.

Prayer: *O God, grant us the faith to show kindness without fear and with abundance in order to glorify you. Amen*

Thought for the day: Today I will choose to show uncommon kindness to someone in need.

Sarah Harris (Tennessee, US)

Trusting the driver

Read 2 Samuel 7:23–29

Trust in the Lord with all your heart and lean not on your own understanding; in all your ways submit to him, and he will make your paths straight.
Proverbs 3:5–6 (NIV)

When I am a passenger in a car, I have noticed that my behaviour varies according to who the driver is. I have felt the need to direct each turn, to tell the driver when the light turns green and even to push my feet to the floor to 'assist' in braking the car.

My compulsion to direct the driver depends on my level of trust. For example, it is very easy to have complete trust in my wife – who can drive any vehicle in any circumstance and capably navigate new cities. Therefore I can totally relax and enjoy the drive whenever she is at the wheel.

It troubles me that I do not always have equal or greater trust in God, my omniscient, omnipresent, omnipotent Creator, Saviour and Lord. Over the years, I have been impatient with God and many times have wanted to step on the accelerator or attempt to turn too soon. I have also put on the brake when it was obvious that God wanted me to go.

God is greater and more trustworthy than any human being in every situation. Knowing this, we can resist leaning on our own understanding and instead trust and submit to God and enjoy the ride.

Prayer: *Dear Lord, help us to remember your continual reassurances to trust you and enjoy the ride. Amen*

Thought for the day: God is the trustworthy driver of my life.

Wayne Schmedel (Oregon, US)

Light from God's word

Read Daniel 2:19–23

Your word is a lamp for my feet, a light on my path.
Psalm 119:105 (NIV)

When my Bible study group began a series on Daniel, the leader suggested that each week we memorise a portion of the passage from today's reading. I groaned inwardly, thinking, memorising is for younger people. My brain doesn't work that way any more. I read scripture daily, and I still remember some verses I learned decades ago, but as for memorising new ones – well, I wasn't optimistic.

Still, having nothing to lose, I gave it my best shot. If I couldn't memorise it, I reasoned, I would still benefit from meditating on it. For the next weeks I began my devotional times by reading each week's section several times, emphasising different words.

I began to notice parallels with my daily life. I meditated on 'He changes times and seasons' (v. 21) in the midst of the glorious autumn foliage. And in the same verse, 'he deposes kings and raises up others' gave me comfort during the latest upheaval in the Middle East. The week when I asked God for wisdom in making an important decision, I was encouraged while repeating, 'you have given me wisdom and power' (v. 23). After five weeks, I was surprised to find that I had memorised the verses.

That was several months ago, and I still begin time with the Lord by repeating this passage. It not only helps me focus on God, but it also reminds me how much his word speaks to our lives.

Prayer: *Dear God, thank you for your word, which lights our path each day. Amen*

Thought for the day: The Bible gives me God's perspective on my life.

Lisa Stackpole (Wisconsin, US)

A piece of cloth

Read Luke 5:33–38

No one tears a piece out of a new garment to patch an old one. Otherwise, they will have torn the new garment, and the patch from the new will not match the old.

Luke 5:36 (NIV)

Our church council decided that the altar cloth needed to be replaced – it was very old and the colours in the embroidery were faded. As I have been doing embroidery since I was a boy, I volunteered to make the new altar cloth.

When I began planning out the project, I remembered the words of Jesus quoted above. It would be impossible to stitch new embroidery on the old cloth. But it was possible to use the old pattern with new thread and new cloth.

As Christians, we use a 2,000-year-old pattern – the gospel – to shape our lives today. The thread and the cloth belong to the present and the gospel is something God gave us long ago – but it is as relevant and true for our lives as ever.

Prayer: *Dear Lord, thank you for your love and grace that make everything new. We pray as Jesus taught us saying, 'Our Father which art in heaven, Hallowed be thy name. Thy kingdom come. Thy will be done in earth, as it is in heaven. Give us this day our daily bread. And forgive us our debts, as we forgive our debtors. And lead us not into temptation, but deliver us from evil: For thine is the kingdom, and the power, and the glory, forever. Amen.'**

Thought for the day: I will seek the truth of God's word as a pattern for my life each day.

Oystein Brinch (Norway)

The thanksgiving choir

Read Nehemiah 12:31–43

Give thanks to the Lord, for he is good; his love endures forever.
Psalm 118:1 (NIV)

Our family has been riding the emotional roller coaster of unemployment and job hunting. The morning I read the Nehemiah passage above, we had been particularly discouraged. My husband and I typically began our day by praying as we walked around our neighbourhood. But that morning we did something different.

Instead of praying for our needs, we decided to join our voices in a 'thanksgiving choir' – much like the choirs that Nehemiah set up. We made no requests, no intercessions, just overflowed with thankfulness. Like a ping-pong game, we batted blessings back and forth.

'Thank you, Lord, for fresh starts and new mercies.' 'Thank you for family.' 'Thank you for a safe neighbourhood.' 'Thank you for meeting our needs.' 'Thank you for hope.'

And on and on it went. We walked for almost an hour and never ran out of blessings for which we were thankful. What began as a discouraging day became a joyful day, simply because we obeyed God's command to give thanks in every situation.

Prayer: *Source of all blessings, thank you for filling our lives with good things, even during difficult times. Help us always to be grateful. Amen*

Thought for the day: Gratitude paves the way for joy.

Lori Hatcher (South Carolina, US)

Why?

Read Job 42:1–5

[Job said,] 'You said, "Listen now, and I will speak; I will question you, and you shall answer me."'
Job 42:4 (NIV)

During an especially stressful time, I found myself waking up in the early hours of the morning for no apparent reason. I grew increasingly frustrated with this, as my mind would start reeling with all the things that created the stress I was feeling. As a result, my body was not getting the rest it needed. Then one morning, as I lay awake pondering why this was happening to me again, I once again asked God to help me get back to sleep. This time, however, I asked God, 'Why?' And I phrased it more like a demand than a question. In the stillness of that night, it was as if God answered me by asking, 'Who hears you? Who helps you? Who heals you?' I was quickly reminded that God always hears me; he always helps me; and he always heals me in a perfect way and time.

How many times do we ask God why our prayers are not being answered? I think we have all identified with Job at some point. When we see, as Job eventually does, that our suffering can lead us to a deeper understanding of God, we can persist in trusting him through all our struggles.

Prayer: *Dear God, help us, like Job, to persist in trusting you. Amen*

Thought for the day: How do I keep my faith in God in challenging times?

Steve McIntosh (Florida, US)

Love poured out

Read Matthew 10:40–42

[Jesus said,] 'Anyone who welcomes you welcomes me, and anyone who welcomes me welcomes the one who sent me.'
Matthew 10:40 (NIV)

As the organiser of a teenage coffee-bar ministry, I have the privilege of spending time each Thursday with some brilliant young people. They're full of life. They brim with passion about their interests and laugh with an abandon that is rare among adults. But each week – over steaming cups of cappuccino – they tell me how domestic abuse, disease, homelessness, the death of loved ones, depression and a slew of other adversities weigh on their hearts. And each time, my heart breaks a little more, too. What can be done about such overwhelming suffering?

As much as I wish I could mend their broken hearts, I can't. Jesus is the only one with the power to do that. But he can use me despite the cracks in my own heart. He can pour out his Spirit through my pouring a fresh cup of coffee or tea and offering a sense of his presence as I sit down to share a listening ear or word of encouragement. Though we can't solve all the world's problems, by being present and willing to listen we can let the love of God flow through us to those around us.

Prayer: *Compassionate God, help us to share your overflowing love with those we meet today. Amen*

Thought for the day: God's love can flow through my brokenness.

Megan L. Anderson (Indiana, US)

The power of prayer

Read Psalm 5:1–7

Listen to the sound of my cry, my King and my God, for to you I pray. O Lord, in the morning you hear my voice; in the morning I plead my case to you, and watch.
Psalm 5:2–3 (NRSV)

Because of the nature of his occupation, my husband always warned us that he could be transferred from one workplace to another at any time. Even so, when it seemed likely that he would be moved, my husband and I were surprised and discouraged. We dreaded having to start again and adjust to a new environment, possible changes in his work, and our children having to deal with a different situation – in short, a whole new life.

We were facing very difficult days so I decided to seek God's guidance, declaring a day of prayer. Often in tears, I asked the Lord to provide us a good place according to his will, despite knowing that the answer might be contrary to my desires. A few days later, I was surprised to learn that the place where my husband worked had set up a new policy of letting each worker choose where their future employment would be.

We will all face major changes in our lives. In this case, God's answer came sooner than expected, and I know that he heard my prayer and will be with us no matter where we go. Today I feel more peaceful about any change that the future may bring.

Prayer: *God of glory, give us faith and strength so that we can view changes as opportunities to grow spiritually. Amen*

Thought for the day: How does God want me to view change?

Clementina Afonso de Sousa (Benguela, Angola)

A shared meal

Read Exodus 16:1–8

Every day, they met together in the temple and ate in their homes. They shared food with gladness and simplicity.
Acts 2:46 (CEB)

During my undergraduate college years, most of my friends belonged to a Jewish congregation that began each weekend with worship and a shared evening meal. I attended several of these Shabbat services, which were led in Hebrew. I did not understand the language or the pattern of worship, but I used the time to pray and came to enjoy the peace and tranquillity of being included in the congregation's worship. Though I had initially felt awkward and out of place, the Shabbat services reminded me of shared meals in my home church, and the worshippers' conviviality revealed to me that these were God's people, too. Although I was far from home and far from the rituals I knew, I enjoyed learning about my friends' faith.

Moses and Aaron had already led the Israelites far from home when the tribe began grumbling about lack of provisions. Their complaints against the Lord had more to do with not trusting God than with the two brothers' poor leadership. Like the Israelites' grumbling, my insecurity at the Shabbat services stemmed from my discomfort with the unfamiliar. Yet when I was receptive to someone else's worship tradition, I experienced God's shalom, which is freely available to any who will accept it.

Prayer: *Dear Lord, teach us to wait with expectant hearts for your blessings to be revealed. In Jesus' name we pray. Amen*

Thought for the day: God delights in my worship, even when I do not know 'the rules'.

Tim Getz (New York, US)

Enough

Read Matthew 6:5–13

One day Jesus was praying in a certain place. When he finished, one of his disciples said to him, 'Lord, teach us to pray.'
Luke 11:1 (NIV)

Like the early disciples, I have struggled to know how to pray. I would hear others pray effortlessly about the state of our world and the needs of others, while I seemed to be at a loss for words. I would chastise myself for prayers that sounded to me like begging or whining. I knew I could pray the prayer Jesus gave his disciples, but it did not seem to be enough.

The fullness of the prayer did not strike me until I read the various 'I am' verses in the book of John: 'I am the true vine' (John 15:1), 'I am the gate' (John 10:7), 'I am the bread of life' (John 6:48). Is Jesus the bread we ask for when we say, 'Give us today our daily bread' (Matthew 6:11)? I began to see the Lord's Prayer in a new light.

Now when I pray for bread, I know I am asking not only for nourishment to stave off physical hunger, but for the Holy Spirit, who feeds the soul. I have ready access to a daily portion of God's bread to sustain my soul. All I have to do is ask.

Prayer: *Gracious God, thank you for giving us the perfect prayer – one that is more than enough for us each day. Amen*

Thought for the day: How will scripture guide my prayers today?

Jeanne Gore (North Carolina, US)

Renewed in spirit

Read 1 Peter 1:3–9

We do not lose heart. Though outwardly we are wasting away, yet inwardly we are being renewed day by day.
2 Corinthians 4:16 (NIV)

In the summer of 2016, disastrous bushfires raged through rural areas of South Australia. Lives were lost, and farms and homes were completely destroyed. Many people not only lost their homes but also their livelihood. People rallied around to help with immediate needs, but many still struggle and some will never completely recover. The land itself was affected. Not a blade of grass was left and the strong wind blew the topsoil away. Huge trees which had taken years to grow were reduced to smouldering ashes.

However, six months later amazing changes started to take place. From the impoverished soil, a few seeds sprouted. Green shoots appeared from old burnt stumps. Refreshing rain was bringing new life. The growth will be slow, but the promise of life is there.

What God can do for land and trees, he will also do for us. In times of stress, when God feels far away and we feel burned out, we can speak honestly to him about our fears. When we accept his love and forgiveness, our spirits will be renewed and growth will come.

Prayer: *Thank you, Lord, for your love and forgiveness in times of stress. Help us to be open to you so that new growth can come. In Jesus' name, we pray. Amen*

Thought for the day: Just as God renews the earth, he can renew my spirit.

Rae Thompson (South Australia, Australia)

Where we are

Read Jeremiah 29:12–14

When you search for me, you will find me; if you seek me with all your heart.
Jeremiah 29:13 (NRSV)

My prayer life shifted when my husband and I had three children in four years. I learned to pray while washing up and on my way to the supermarket. Most of those prayers were as simple as 'Help!' and, faithfully, God heard each one of them. Even simple prayers are powerful because God meets us where we are.

I can see this in the life of Susanna Wesley, who raised 19 children. Two of those children were John Wesley, founder of the Methodist Church, and Charles Wesley, a powerful evangelist and amazing hymn writer. Living in the 1600s, Susanna educated her children, cooked and did everything in between. But Susanna was determined to include time with God in her busy schedule; and the same God who met her in a constantly busy life will meet each of us wherever we are.

Even someone who has never experienced little children running around the house all day knows what it is to live a hectic life. No matter how busy our schedules are, God knows where we are and can meet us there through prayer. He cares about what concerns us and wants to hear about what's filling our hearts and minds. Each day, we can all resolve to set aside some time to connect with God through prayer.

Prayer: *Loving God, thank you for listening to our prayers. As we search for you, may we be enveloped by your amazing love. Amen*

Thought for the day: God is near me every day – 'a very present help' (Psalm 46:1, KJV).

Cintia Listenbee (Texas, US)

PRAYER FOCUS: MOTHERS OF SMALL CHILDREN

Playlist

Read Psalm 32:6–11

Do not fear, for I am with you; do not be dismayed, for I am your God. I will strengthen you and help you; I will uphold you with my righteous right hand.

Isaiah 41:10 (NIV)

I sat in the surgeon's office, confident that God was in charge and that the biopsy report would be good. Then the surgeon came in, took my hand and told me the news I had never expected to hear. I had a particularly aggressive type of breast cancer and would need an operation, chemotherapy and radiation. But, he added, 'We have caught it early so we are going to expect a cure.'

My whole life went into a tailspin. During the following weeks I dutifully walked through a maze of doctor's appointments, tests and scans, trying to fit them around my job. Fear and worry were my constant companions. The day of my operation was almost a relief.

The months ahead were definitely not easy, but during that time God spoke to me through song, and I knew I was not alone. I was walking through deep waters, but he was with me every step of the way. I developed a playlist that I listened to over and over again, allowing God's grace and love to replace fear with hope. As my treatment was healing my body, music was healing my soul.

Even today, two years cancer free, when I hear some of the songs from my playlist I remember all I went through. But more importantly, I am assured that God will be with me no matter what lies ahead.

Prayer: *God of all comfort, thank you for being with us during hard times. Help us always to rely on your grace. Amen*

Thought for the day: No matter how deep the water is, God is with me.

Kim Sisk (Oklahoma, US)

Powerful words

Read James 3:3–13

Gracious words are a honeycomb, sweet to the soul and healing to the bones.

Proverbs 16:24 (NIV)

Words are powerful. When I was a child, I was never chosen to play in the school sports teams and I suffered from the hurtful words others said to me. Although I tried to strengthen myself in the face of their bullying, still their words affected me deeply. Over time, I became angry, quiet and withdrawn.

This experience made me consider carefully how I use my words. If I do not have something good to say to others, I try to refrain from saying anything. Better still, I can find words that encourage and build up others. But at times, even with our best intentions, people are hurt by our words – sometimes without our even knowing it.

So, our words must have their foundation in love. The Bible verse quoted above is a good reminder. Pleasant words can bring encouragement to the soul, and even healing to the body. All that we say should be motivated by good will and a desire to love the other person.

Prayer: *O Lord, grant us gracious words to bless the people around us. Amen*

Thought for the day: Today I will show God's love by speaking words of encouragement.

Moisés Abdon Coppe (Minas Gerais, Brazil)

A new friend

Read Luke 12:6–7

I have called you by name; you are mine.
Isaiah 43:1 (CEB)

At times I hear my colleagues chatting with the cleaners in our building. I used to feel a little uncomfortable and tongue-tied in these moments because they reminded me of my privilege as a person who works in an office and who has her waste bin emptied for her. Instead of making conversation like my colleagues did, I used to only mumble, 'How are you?' and 'Thank you.' One day, one of the cleaners took the initiative to talk to me. Now, every day he greets me by name and makes me smile. He is kind and funny and asks about my friends and the work I do. In return, I wave and say hello – asking him how his day is going and telling him that I hope I will see him the next day. This friendship is a gift of God's grace that I neither expected nor initiated.

My new friend's kindness reminds me of the importance of venturing out of my comfort zone to seek relationships with the people around me. As he and I talk, I am reminded that being recognised, called by name and appreciated are blessings that I receive from God and from others. When we remember that God calls us by name and seeks a relationship with us, we, in turn, can offer the gifts of appreciation and recognition to those around us.

Prayer: *Loving God, open our eyes and ears to those around us. Remind us to call others by name as you have called us. Amen*

Thought for the day: Who is God calling me to befriend?

Joanna Bradley (Tennessee, US)

Daily blessings

Read Numbers 6:22–27

Set your minds on things that are above, not on things that are on earth, for you have died, and your life is hidden with Christ in God.
Colossians 3:2–3 (NRSV)

While dealing with the effects of cancer treatment, I would often find myself numbering the days: only 25 more days of radiation... only two more days of chemotherapy. During this difficult time, our family was blessed with many beautiful get-well cards and plenty of meals and prayers from church members and friends. However, I often failed to see these gifts as blessings from God. I thought that I could count myself blessed only after I was totally finished with all my treatments and everything had returned to normal. Now, I realise that when I was totally focused on the future, I missed the blessings of each day.

As Christians, we know that today our lives are 'hidden with God'. Our lives aren't perfect, but when Jesus comes again, we will be made new and every tear will be wiped away from our eyes. God promises that one glorious day we will see clearly what is difficult for us to understand now. In addition to this future hope, today's quoted scripture verses remind us that we have already 'died'. God has already raised us to new life with Christ, and every day we can experience his blessings. As Christians, not only do we have the hope of a glorious future to look forward to, but we are also promised a new and abundant life for today (see John 10:10.)

Prayer: *Gracious God, remind us of your blessings today, and strengthen us by hope in your promise for tomorrow. Amen*

Thought for the day: Instead of worrying about the future, I'll praise God for today's blessings.

Geoffrey L. Snook (Kansas, US)

Many ways

Read Matthew 25:14–30

There are different kinds of service, but the same Lord. There are different kinds of working, but in all of them and in everyone it is the same God at work.
1 Corinthians 12:5–6 (NIV)

For a long time, I wanted to participate in the ministry of my church, but I didn't know what I could do. I don't have a good singing voice and am not able to play music. I didn't think I would be very good at welcoming people to the services. I didn't have the ability to interpret the sermon for others. I was confused. What could I do as my ministry?

Then, I felt God speaking into my heart, 'Lina, you can write articles for the church magazine.' Without hesitation, I began writing and sending in articles regularly and some of them appeared in the magazine. Some of my friends told me that they were blessed by my writing. I thanked God for this opportunity to serve.

Ministry is not merely serving inside the church. God has many ways for us to serve – caring for children, elderly people, widows or for someone in need. We also can be good listeners. When we serve God with all our heart, we will shine like stars in the world. Finally we will hear the King say to us, 'Well done, good and faithful servant!' (Matthew 25:21, NIV).

Prayer: *Beloved God, open our eyes and hearts so we can see the opportunities you give us to serve others. Amen*

Thought for the day: God is not concerned with how big my ministry is, but with my sincere service.

Linawati Santoso (East Java, Indonesia)

Rejection

Read Galatians 6:7–10

Let us not grow weary in doing what is right, for we will reap at harvest time, if we do not give up.
Galatians 6:9 (NRSV)

The email stung. Magazine editors had rejected my devotional writing submission. I had put a lot of time and thought into that piece; I believed in my words. I tried to imagine the editors' viewpoint and to sense the challenging decisions they make each day reading endless similar submissions.

Some days I grow weary in my writing. I think, 'Why should I continue?' But then I remind myself of the verse quoted above. Giving up is a sign of my unwillingness to be led by the Lord. Perhaps God is stirring me with these words from Isaiah 28:16: 'See, I lay a stone in Zion, a tested stone, a precious cornerstone for a sure foundation; the one who relies on it will never be stricken with panic' (NIV). While rejection might fracture my trust in the cornerstone, failure provides an opportunity to learn.

On those disappointing days when rejection challenges us, we don't have to panic. Instead, we can trust in God's sure foundation where we find the strength of the Lord ready to push us beyond the sting of rejection.

Prayer: *Heavenly Father, when we encounter the frustration of rejection, help us to return to your sure foundation. As Jesus taught us, we pray, 'Father, hallowed be your name, your kingdom come. Give us each day our daily bread. Forgive us our sins, for we also forgive everyone who sins against us. And lead us not into temptation.'* Amen*

Thought for the day: Rejection is an opportunity to rebuild my trust in God.

Bill Pike (Virginia, US)

PRAYER FOCUS: WRITERS
*Luke 11:2–4, NIV

Sacred silence

Read 1 Kings 19:11–13

After the earthquake [there was] a fire, but the Lord was not in the fire; and after the fire a sound of sheer silence.
1 Kings 19:12 (NRSV)

As a girl, I expected God's voice to come booming from parted clouds, and when it never happened, I just assumed that God did not care about me. Today's reading, however, reminds us that God often speaks to us not in earth-shattering ways but in stillness and quiet. It was through 'a sound of sheer silence' that Elijah heard God's voice.

When my grandmother passed away, I could not stop crying. Wanting to be alone, I hiked up a mountain close to where I lived. I sat on a rock some distance away from the main path and the distractions of modern life. There, I just let the tears flow. In that time of grief, I knew that God was near. In the silence, he comforted me through the warmth of the sun. In the silence, he renewed me with the coolness of the wind, and in the silence, I sensed him saying, 'You are not alone. This is not the end. You will see her again. I love you.'

In the silence, God's voice becomes clear. He wants to show love for us – to respond to our struggles, joys, frustrations, dreams and all that is in our hearts. In the silence, God speaks.

Prayer: *Dear God, help us to quiet our hearts so that we may hear you more clearly. Amen*

Thought for the day: I can hear God's loving voice in moments of silence.

Carrell Jamilano (California, US)

Nudges from God

Read Proverbs 3:27–29

Don't withhold good from someone who deserves it, when it is in your power to do so.
Proverbs 3:27 (CEB)

Our friend Bill had cancer surgery and was to begin radiation treatment soon after. Instead, Bill had to be admitted twice to intensive care and undergo five more operations. Bill's wife, Julie, emailed prayer requests and updates and made daily long drives to the hospital. Exhaustion eventually overwhelmed her.

After reading Julie's latest email, I asked God, 'What can I do to help?' Then a thought crossed my mind. I could ask Julie if she wanted to stay with us. My next thought was that she was already staying with friends. I told my husband, and he felt we should offer our home anyway. As I talked to Julie, she started crying. 'My friends just told me they are going on holiday,' she said, 'so I felt I would have to leave.' I had heard stories of needs being met at just the right time and I had always wondered how that happened. In this case, my thought to invite Julie into our home was so powerful that it was as if God had spoken it out loud.

God works in as many ways as there are people who are willing to act upon divine prompting. When God nudges us to help someone, we can take every opportunity to serve those around us.

Prayer: *Dear God, show us people who need our help today, and give us the courage to act. Amen*

Thought for the day: What has God given me that I can share with someone else?

Pamela Rosales (Oregon, US)

Drops of paint

Read Titus 2:11–14

[Jesus Christ] gave himself… to purify for himself a people that are his very own, eager to do what is good.
Titus 2:14 (NIV)

The wooden stepladder I had borrowed was old, but it would do the job as I painted the ceiling in my house. Distracted by the task at hand, I took several hours to notice that the ladder was covered by drops of paint. Some were large and others tiny, but hardly a patch of original wood could be seen under the rainbow of colours.

It was not hard to see how these layers had been deposited. In fact, I contributed a number of my own white dots that day, but they were few compared to the thousands already there. It must have taken many years to develop such a thick coat of paint drops.

As I painted the ceiling that day, I realised that this was a picture of my life with Christ. Just as that ladder collected droplets in the presence of a painter, my character will show that I have been with the Master. I hope that my attitude is more understanding and hopeful while my actions grow in gentleness and compassion. Peace and forgiveness will mark my relationships as I forgive, just as Jesus forgave me. After all, he purifies us so that we may be 'eager to do what is good'.

Prayer: *Lord Jesus, help us to act more like you so that, little by little, people will see more of you in us. Amen*

Thought for the day: My character reflects my relationship with Christ.

Troy Dennis (Manitoba, Canada)

Baskets of blessings

Read Psalm 100:3–5

Rejoice always, pray without ceasing, give thanks in all circumstances.
1 Thessalonians 5:16–18 (NRSV)

When I was a young mother, one of my least-favourite tasks was folding the clean clothes for my family. All those baskets heaped with mounds of little shirts, trousers, dresses, socks and baby blankets would take ages to fold. Just looking at them made me miserable. Then one day in the middle of my grumbling, a thought settled in my mind. What if, instead of viewing this task as a chore, I could see it as one of God's blessings? What if I prayed for each member of my family while I folded their clean clothes?

And so I began. The blankets reminded me that God's love surrounded and comforted each child. Each T-shirt was a prayer for a loving heart. Even the endless socks, which never seemed to come out even, became a prayer that the feet they covered would walk in God's path. Before I knew it, all those baskets were empty; the bed was full of neatly folded clothes and my heart overflowed with gratitude for all of God's blessings.

My children are now grown and have families of their own, and folding laundry is still not my favourite task. But when I remember to adjust my spiritual attitude, the baskets of drudgery are transformed into baskets of blessings.

Prayer: *Dear Lord, help us to recognise and give thanks for the blessings you surround us with every day. Amen*

Thought for the day: Which everyday task can become my time for prayer?

Nancy Clark (Michigan, US)

Yet I will rejoice in the Lord

Read Habakkuk 3:17–19

I have learned the secret of being content in any and every situation.
Philippians 4:12 (NIV)

When we went through a particularly difficult time with our son recently, facing aggression, suicide threats and deep despair, and at the same time my husband's health deteriorated, I emailed many Christian friends, asking for prayer. One friend reminded me that the sacrifice of praise allows the Holy Spirit to fill our lives, and that praising God in all circumstances can be very empowering. She gently exhorted me to try it.

So the next morning I came up with a lot of things for which I praised God: my three wonderful sisters, the riotous colour in the hanging baskets, full cupboards, freedom to pray in safety and even a favourite TV programme. It isn't hard to find things to be thankful for, and though I know I fail to do it all the time, it is a prayer practice well worth taking up.

Of course, the real challenge is to praise God for the difficult situations we find ourselves in, which seem contrary to his plans for us. I'm still working on that one! To paraphrase Habakkuk: 'Though my son is deeply depressed, though my husband's health is poor and his disability increases, though there is little in the bank and we have a huge mortgage to pay, "yet I will rejoice"…'

Prayer: *Lord, help me to thank you in all the circumstances of my life and to trust that you are there in the midst of them. Amen*

Thought for the day: What can I thank God for today?

Sue Richards (Buckinghamshire, England)

God's faithful provision

Read Philippians 4:18–20

My God shall supply all your need according to his riches in glory by Christ Jesus.

Philippians 4:19 (KJV)

When my late husband Charles and I married, we committed ourselves completely to God by praying from the Methodist Covenant Prayer: 'Let me be full, let me be empty; let me have all things, let me have nothing. We freely and heartily yield all things to your pleasure and disposal.'

Having a child each year while Charles finished his theological studies meant that money was tight, but God provided in many ways, including money left in a blank envelope in our letter box. When Charles received a scholarship to do a Ph.D. in Canberra, life was easier and more pleasant. Our fourth child was born during our first year in a parish in Newcastle and I needed a lot of bed rest. But again God provided for us through a good friend in the church who helped by cleaning our home each week.

In 1974, while we were living in Brisbane, my husband suggested that I finish the degree I had begun in 1955. I was afraid of failure, but many things came together to make study possible – the children being at school, the government temporarily removing university fees, living close to the university. Once again God had provided for us! I am convinced that when we step out in faith, God will provide for us in unexpected ways.

Prayer: *Heavenly Father, help us to have the courage to follow your will for our lives, trusting you to provide what we need to serve you. Amen*

Thought for the day: God can answer my prayers in unexpected ways.

Patricia Noller (Queensland, Australia)

One day at a time

Read Ecclesiastes 3:1–11

There is a time for everything, and a season for every activity under the heavens.
Ecclesiastes 3:1 (NIV)

When I was first diagnosed with cancer, my stomach knotted up with fear. What type of surgery would I have? How much chemotherapy would I need, if any? When would radiation begin? One morning, feeling overwhelmed, I cried out to God, 'I can't do all of this!'

Reading the passage above from Ecclesiastes reminded me that I didn't have to complete everything all at once. Our ever-present Counsellor, the Holy Spirit, came alongside me, and I heard a whisper in my heart. 'You only need to cope with one thing at a time.' My shoulders relaxed and a smile spread across my face.

Day by day, I spoke with doctors and appointments were made for scans, tests and operations. Week by week, I ticked appointments and procedures off the list. Finally, after a few months, I started on the road to recovery.

That stage of my life was very challenging, yet I felt God with me each moment. I don't know what joys and struggles the future will bring, but I do have peace in my heart. I trust that our Sovereign Lord has ordained a time for everything.

Prayer: *Dear Father, help us rest in you, knowing that you are with us in the details of each day. Amen*

Thought for the day: I can rely on God to help me through challenges one step at a time.

Debbie Jones Warren (California, US)

Watering the fields

Read Deuteronomy 10:12–22

Be doers of the word, and not merely hearers who deceive themselves.
James 1:22 (NRSV)

Farming on the high plains is a daunting task. With little rain, hot summers and cold winters, growing anything other than weeds can be hard work. Fortunately, in many areas we are able to use underground water for irrigation. The green circles that the sprayers make tell it all. Where the land is watered you can grow almost anything; where it's not, you can't grow much at all.

I used this analogy in my Bible class at church when I was teaching about how the apostles carried their message to new lands. Our whole community has benefited from our active and mission-minded church. From members delivering meals to older people, to those collecting donations for those who have suffered disasters, we give of ourselves in time, money and effort to improve the lives of those around us – whoever they may be and from wherever they may come. To me, this way of putting our faith into action is an essential part of what it means to be truly Christian.

Unfortunately, the world always has had, and probably always will have, barren patches. But if we can make even one patch greener than it has been, then we are truly being Christ's hands and feet in the world.

Prayer: *Dear Lord, help us to remember that our actions and not our words alone proclaim your power and grace to the world. Amen*

Thought for the day: God visits the church but works in the world.

Mark A. Carter (Oregon, US)

Words that heal

Read Isaiah 53:1–10

Surely he took up our pain and bore our suffering.
Isaiah 53:4 (NIV)

Twelve years ago I was diagnosed with chronic malaria. Every week I had to go to the hospital to receive treatment, and I felt in deep despair. Then, one week, a work colleague invited me to attend a service at his church. At first I was reluctant, but my husband convinced me to go. When the service started, the words of the hymns deeply touched my heart. Then I heard the local pastor preaching on Isaiah 53, about how the Lord heals all our diseases. From that moment I noticed a difference in my life and gave myself completely to God, having learned to pray in a new way.

Since then, I have been praying about my distress and my worry has disappeared. Often my prayers have been answered. God helped me to keep my mind and my heart focused on Jesus Christ. My illness was cured with the help of medication. But nothing was more effective in pulling me out of the darkness than the clear words of God.

Prayer: *Thank you, Lord, for words that bring healing and illuminate our lives. Amen*

Thought for the day: Scripture offers me hope in times of trouble.

Madalena Manuel Simão (Luanda, Angola)

Faithfulness

Read Psalm 57:8–11

The steadfast love of the Lord never ceases, his mercies never come to an end; they are new every morning; great is your faithfulness.
Lamentations 3:22–23 (NRSV)

Every morning I watch as the sky begins to lighten on our farm. When I can see the sun's brilliant rays skimming across the fields, I know it is time to open the barn. The peacocks scream from their high roost in the trees, alerting the birds in the barn that I am coming.

The geese honk impatiently for their liberty. They do not know that I am protecting them from night-time predators. They do not understand that everything I do to look after them is for their sake. But I am faithful anyway.

As I open the barn door, the birds burst forth, tumbling over each other to be first at the water trough. They plunge their heads deep under the water's surface, causing the water to wash over them as they tremble with glee. I take great pleasure in faithfully caring for them.

In a similar way, God faithfully cares for us. He protects us whether we understand or not, whether we credit our Creator or not. He never wearies of the task, and he never oversleeps or becomes ill. God takes pleasure in us. He is faithful.

Prayer: *Faithful God, we praise your name. May we always be faithful to you. Amen*

Thought for the day: God delights in caring for me.

Sharon B. Capron (Oklahoma, US)

Faith training

Read 1 Timothy 4:7–10

While physical training is of some value, godliness is valuable in every way.
1 Timothy 4:8 (NRSV)

In my college gym class, I learned that three main types of weight training correspond to three different goals: using low weight for a long time produces muscular endurance; medium weight for a shorter amount of time enlarges muscles; and a lot of weight in short bursts builds muscle density. I realised that people could be strong in dramatically different ways. For example, a spindly but sure-footed marathon runner trains just as hard as the stout body-builder, even though the two appear to be opposites at first glance.

Since taking that course I've become increasingly absorbed in my own physical training, but the results have surprised me. Rather than bulking up or slimming down, I instead found myself becoming more at home in the type of body I already had. In addition, I discovered myself drawing closer to God through daily spiritual practice and found a greater awareness of God's presence.

We who belong to the body of Christ have all 'worked out' through our experience of trials and the pursuit of knowledge. Some of us have gained scholarly strength, while others have the endurance of faith produced by personal encounters with God. Even though some do weight training and others run marathons, we all draw strength from the one true God.

Prayer: *Dear Lord, just as we thank you for our unique spiritual strengths, we ask you to help us love others for theirs. Amen*

Thought for the day: Physical fitness gains eternal value when it promotes spiritual fitness.

Jeff Grogan (Indiana, US)

God's eternal supply

Read Isaiah 40:27–31

Do you not know? Have you not heard? The Lord is the everlasting God, the Creator of the ends of the earth. He will not grow tired or weary, and his understanding no one can fathom.
Isaiah 40:28 (NIV)

I live in an area where storms, called Nor'easters, ride up the coast and hit us hard. When such a storm is predicted, people stock up on essentials like bread, water and petrol. Often the demand is so great that there are empty shelves in supermarkets or signs at petrol stations indicating that the fuel supplies have run out.

As I was thinking about this in the midst of a storm, I remembered that God is always rich in supplies. His love is eternal and his mercy and strength never run out.

At times I have underestimated God's resources. In my younger days, I was often afraid to pray when I could not imagine an answer to my prayer. I am beginning to realise that I don't have to worry about whether a prayer could be answered. Instead I need only to trust in the One whose supply of love, mercy and strength is abundant and always available.

Prayer: *Dear Lord, thank you for faithfully loving us. Help us to share your gifts of mercy and forgiveness with others. Amen*

Thought for the day: God's love, forgiveness and mercy are always free and abundant.

Lin Daniels (Massachusetts, US)

Healing by grace

Read Romans 8:37–39

[The Lord said,] 'I will never leave you nor forsake you.'
Joshua 1:5 (NIV)

Already a cardiac patient for 17 years, I began experiencing pain that was much more severe than ever before. Ultimately I had to be taken to a specialised-care hospital in our capital city of Bhubaneswar. It turned out that I had suffered three heart attacks, any one of which could have been fatal. When I was taken on a stretcher for an angiogram, my mind was filled with many questions but also a favourite scripture verse: 'I will never leave you nor forsake you.' Immediately I felt comfort in knowing that the Lord was with me.

The discovery of three blocked arteries required immediate angioplasty procedures. Through all of this, God provided medical professionals, medicine and money. The church and other friends and relations were praying for me. I have always believed that healing comes from God, and after a few days in the hospital I returned home – a living testimony to being healed by the grace of God.

Each one of us may face very difficult and painful times, but according to the Bible, God will never leave us nor forsake us. Based on a lifetime of experience with the Lord, I can join the apostle Paul in saying, 'Neither height nor depth, nor anything else in all creation, will be able to separate us from the love of God that is in Christ Jesus our Lord' (Romans 8:39, NIV).

Prayer: *Dear God, thank you for being with us during the most crucial times in life. Help us to grow in faith. Amen*

Thought for the day: God will never leave me nor forsake me.

Tarak Kumar Pramanik (Odisha, India)

Last in line

Read 1 Samuel 16:1–12

People look at the outward appearance, but the Lord looks at the heart.
1 Samuel 16:7 (NIV)

I must admit that Carl wasn't my first choice. At the time, he wasn't even on my radar. I had requested a brown, female bulldog. Unfortunately, the brown beauty died only a couple of days after birth. Being eager for a new bulldog puppy, I didn't hesitate when the breeder sent me a picture of a small fawn-coloured male. Little did I know that this precious puppy – my second choice – would have such an impact on my life.

Some of us have felt the effects of being a second or even last choice. I find comfort in the fact that even David's own father failed to consider him as a candidate to be the next king. Jesse presented Samuel with all his sons except David. But God told Samuel that David was the chosen one, that the Lord does not judge by the outward appearance, but by the heart.

I have definitely been guilty of looking only at outward appearance. It is human nature to gravitate towards people who are like us in appearance or character. But if we are to emulate Jesus, we will look beyond the exterior and seek out the heart. I am so thankful that God has given me friends from different ethnic and social backgrounds who are also seeking God's heart. But most importantly, I believe that I will continue to be blessed with the assurance that God has chosen me.

Prayer: *Dear Lord, help us to look beyond people's appearance, ethnicity or background and see them as you do. Amen*

Thought for the day: Every day I will try to view people the way God does.

Cora Hawkins Darrah (North Carolina, US)

We will do it

Read 1 Chronicles 28:1–10

Serve [God] with wholehearted devotion and with a willing mind.
1 Chronicles 28:9 (NIV)

In the weekly prayer meeting at our church, one man in the group often closes his prayer with the words, 'Please tell us what to do, and we will do it.' Those words remind me of what David told his son Solomon – that the Lord had chosen Solomon to build the temple. With that responsibility there came also this admonition from David: 'Be strong and do the work.'

David told his son to 'acknowledge the God of your father' and to consider carefully what it means that 'the Lord has chosen you'. Since the Lord searches the heart and understands every motive, Solomon knew that he had an awesome responsibility.

But we also have responsibilities that God has given us. If we are going to ask God to guide our life, then we had better be prepared to do whatever he calls us to do 'with wholehearted devotion and with a willing mind'. My friend has the right idea: First we find out what God wants us to do – then we do it.

Prayer: *Dear Father, give us wholehearted devotion and willing minds to serve where, when and how you call us. Amen*

Thought for the day: When God calls me, I will follow wholeheartedly.

Roger Palms (Florida, US)

God loves me!

Read Lamentations 3:18–26

[The Lord your God] will create calm with his love; he will rejoice over you with singing.
Zephaniah 3:17 (CEB)

As young girls, my friends and I would often pick wildflowers and begin to pluck the petals off, one by one. With each petal, we would quote alternately, 'He loves me' and 'He loves me not.' This was to determine whether or not our latest beau loved us. Of course, we always hoped that the last petal would end with the affirmative.

A while back, I had been through some difficult health challenges and my emotions were at a pretty low point. I began to feel negative and unlovable. One day, I remembered the 'petal' game. I felt that God was showing me that I was playing the same, silly game concerning his love for me. I was determining how much I thought he loved me based on my own changing moods. Of course, this is not reality. God's love for us never wavers. I immediately felt reassured of his steadfast, unchanging and totally reliable love.

As we come to know God better, we can be sure that the truth is never, 'God loves me not' but always, 'God loves me!'

Prayer: *Dear Father, thank you for loving us always and forever, in spite of what our world or our emotions sometimes tell us. Amen*

Thought for the day: No matter how I feel, God loves me.

Belle Todd (Texas, US)

Spirit surfing?

Read Romans 8:26–28

All who are led by the Spirit of God are children of God.
Romans 8:14 (NRSV)

Augusta, Australia, is a great place for windsurfing enthusiasts. It is windy and exposed, making it ideal for this sporting activity that appeals to the young, the very fit and those with the right equipment, training and free-spirited attitude. As many as 30 people may be windsurfing at a time. All rely on the same wind, but they follow very different trajectories and patterns across the water. Some surfers are able to get their boards airborne as they manoeuvre their sails, skimming across the waves and making use of the wind currents.

As Christians, we too make use of the wind – the Holy Spirit – to propel us along God's path. The Spirit empowers us to perform all sorts of wonders for the cause of Christ. But sometimes we lack the commitment or the willingness to be blown in a new direction. We would rather choose a path safe from strong winds or sudden twists and turns. But what exhilaration and joys are we missing out on when we choose the safe way, rather than the way of the Spirit?

Prayer: *Dear Jesus, help us to trust God implicitly, the way you did, so that we will be ready to allow the Spirit to direct our paths. Amen*

Thought for the day: How am I obedient to the leading of the Spirit?

Meg Mangan (New South Wales, Australia)

Praying for one another

Read James 5:13–16

I thank my God every time I remember you. In all my prayers for all of you, I always pray with joy.
Philippians 1:3–4 (NIV)

'Do you pray? Would you like me to pray for you and me?' I was lying awaiting an operation as I heard these words from my surgeon. I assured him of my gratitude, and he prayed; and I entered the operating theatre with peace and assurance. Since that time I have often thought of the way my life has been blessed through the prayers of others. Parents, teachers, people in churches and my work colleagues – the list goes on and on. Their prayers have been a vital part of my life.

Those memories cause me to realise how important it is for me to be part of that ministry of intercession. All around us people need God's touch and long to know that others care for them and are petitioning him on their behalf. If we open our eyes and ears, we will see their needs, which he supplies through his people. Our offer of prayer can provide hope and can assure them that they do not face their trials alone. We may not be able to meet all their needs, but we can pray. And our God will hear and answer those prayers.

Prayer: *Dear Lord God, show us the needs of those around us so that we can give hope and peace to others as we serve and pray for them. In Jesus' name. Amen*

Thought for the day: 'I'm praying for you' assures someone that they are being cared for.

Robert J. Beyer (Florida, US)

PRAYER FOCUS: SURGEONS

Keep pedalling

Read Isaiah 43:18–21

I can do all things through Christ which strengtheneth me.
Philippians 4:13 (KJV)

Several years ago, I invested in a new bike. I rode around my neighbourhood, occasionally down to a nearby park, sometimes to my voluntary job at my church, to the bank and once for a Sunday service. I noticed that while riding, although I needed to be mindful of what was behind me, too much glancing backwards slowed me down and could be dangerous.

Similarly the journey of life requires us to keep moving forward. Dwelling too long on past disappointments, regrets and mistakes can impede God's purpose for our lives. This is by no means easy. It takes physical, mental and spiritual energy to let go and look to the future. For an example of how to do this, we can look to Jesus who spent time in prayer and taught us to do the same. He knew his Father would see us through. God beckons us to keep pedalling. The answers to our prayers could be just around the corner.

Prayer: *Dear God, strengthen us in mind, body and spirit to serve you and to not grow weary in doing good. Amen*

Thought for the day: With God's help, I can let go of the past and move forward.

Nancy Latina (Ohio, US)

The eyes of our hearts

Read Ephesians 1:17–21

I pray that the eyes of your heart may be enlightened.
Ephesians 1:18 (NIV)

Some years ago my wife and I visited the Grand Canyon. We had seen photographs of it before we went and so we knew exactly what to expect. However, when we walked up to the edge of the canyon and looked out across the vast expanse before our eyes, I just said 'Wow!' No photograph or video could do justice to the magnificent sight before us.

We all have our own impression of what God is like. No doubt it is shaped by what we have heard and read, as well as by our experiences of life. But then something can happen that suddenly opens our eyes to see the truth about God in a new and vivid way. Suddenly he seems more real to us, and the truths that we believe about him come to life. This is the work of the Holy Spirit who, Jesus told us, reveals to us the truth about God.

In today's reading Paul refers to 'the eyes of your heart', by which he means our spiritual sight. Just as many of us need to wear glasses to be able to see clearly with our physical eyes, so our spiritual eyes also need to be enlightened. So we make Paul's prayer our own, that the Holy Spirit may open our eyes to see new truths about God.

Prayer: *Heavenly Father, send out your light and your truth; let them lead me (Psalm 43:3, NRSV). Amen*

Thought for the day: Today I will seek for new truths in God's word.

David Butterfield (North Yorkshire, England)

God's call

Read Joshua 1:5–9

Be strong and courageous. Do not be afraid; do not be discouraged, for the Lord your God will be with you wherever you go.
Joshua 1:9 (NIV)

I grew up going to church with my parents every Sunday. At first I did not understand anything at all and thought that church was only for adults. But as I grew, I began to realise the value of attending church.

When I accepted Jesus into my heart, my life changed completely. My faith in Christ strengthened, and I received the call to share the gospel through choral singing. I started singing and improved quickly. I even recorded three albums. This resulted in invitations to sing in many countries such as Angola, Zimbabwe, Kenya, Norway, the United States and Mexico. I had never imagined that one day I would be singing all over the world or that my music would be heard even in places I've never visited.

When we obey God's call, we receive power from the Holy Spirit, and the Lord will do great things in our lives. We all have received special gifts from God. We can use our gifts to serve our neighbours and to spread the word of God to the ends of the earth.

Prayer: *Dear Lord, teach us to praise you in spirit and in truth. We pray in Jesus' name. Amen*

Thought for the day: What spiritual gift can I share with the world?

Palmira Kilende (São Paulo, Brazil)

Clear vision

Read Psalm 148:1–14

You shall go out in joy, and be led back in peace; the mountains and the hills before you shall burst into song, and all the trees of the field shall clap their hands.
Isaiah 55:12 (NRSV)

Several years ago, after returning from my evening walk, I composed these words for my journal: 'I saw a tree today, straight and tall, rooted in the clay. Its branches spread beneath the sky, praising God – and so shall I.' When I walk that path, I often think or recite these words.

Recently, I had cataract surgery on both my eyes. The change to my vision had been gradual, and I had not realised how blurred it had become. Now I am once again able to see the magnificent beauty of the tree that inspired me to write those words.

Reflecting on this change, I realised that in the same way that my vision gradually changed, my spiritual vision can also become blurred. Just as I finally decided to have my eyes examined and successfully treated, so too does my spiritual vision need continued treatment. With the Holy Spirit's guidance and as I join with fellow believers in worship, prayer and Bible study, my spiritual vision will stay focused on God's love and grace, and I will clearly see the redeeming love of Christ.

Prayer: *Dear God, thank you for your gift of Christ Jesus and for the Holy Spirit who lives within us. Amen*

Thought for the day: Spending quiet moments alone with God keeps my spiritual vision clear.

Charles F. Holm (Minnesota, US)

Compassionate giving

Read Mark 12:41–44

Everyone should give whatever they have decided in their heart. They shouldn't give with hesitation or because of pressure. God loves a cheerful giver.
2 Corinthians 9:7 (CEB)

Our minister recently challenged us to discover the depths of generosity and the blessings of giving. Every day for a fortnight, we were given a new task designed to help us discover the gift of generosity.

During this experience, I remembered that in the early years of my parents' marriage, they struggled financially due to a meagre income, education expenses, family illness and running an old car. At a church prayer meeting, a gentleman stood and told of a family in the community which was experiencing great difficulties and needed help. My father had hardly any money in his pocket, but with a loving and generous heart, he contributed all of it to the needy family. The following day, he was shocked to learn that the money had been collected for us, for his family.

I am thankful for my father's example of sacrificial giving. Greater still is the ultimate example of generosity demonstrated by our Lord Jesus Christ. When opportunities arise to contribute time or resources, I reflect on these examples of selflessness and strive to give with a joyful and grateful heart.

Prayer: *Generous God, help us never to take for granted all that comes from you. Give us generous hearts as we serve others in your name. Amen*

Thought for the day: When I acknowledge God's blessings, I can be more generous.

Joy Freeman Buff (North Carolina, US)

The power of Jesus

Read Luke 5:12–15

The news about [Jesus] spread all the more, so that crowds of people came to hear him and to be healed of their illnesses.
Luke 5:15 (NIV)

In today's reading, we find a man suffering with a painful and (at the time) incurable disease. The effects of leprosy were severe and evident to all. Those who suffered from it endured not only physical pain but isolation from their families and communities. When Jesus healed those with leprosy, he showed that his power could overcome even this affliction.

The presence of Jesus was good news to the man with leprosy. Simply because the Lord was there, the man rediscovered hope – something he had lost long before. 'Lord, if you are willing, you can make me clean,' was his cry. His lying prostrate on the ground showed his deep suffering and sorrow. And the man had reason to feel that way. But at the same time, he believed that Jesus could heal him.

This remains good news for us today. In the presence of the Lord, we can always hope. Whatever problems, pain or issues we bring to him, Jesus has the power to make us whole.

Prayer: *Dear God, thank you for your healing power in our lives. Grant us strength in the face of life's challenges. Amen*

Thought for the day: I can find hope for healing in Jesus.

António Wilson (Inhambane, Mozambique)

Special gifts

Read 1 Peter 4:8–11

Each of you should use whatever gift you have received to serve others, as faithful stewards of God's grace in its various forms.
1 Peter 4:10 (NIV)

My mother had the gift of hospitality. Even when we had very little money, she would whip up a spaghetti dinner with lots of steaming pasta and tasty sauce. Then she would make a big green salad and a lovely cake. At times we would have as many as 15 people squeezed into our tiny home for a meal. I've tried to imitate her way of entertaining people, but I feel inadequate. I admire my mother's way of showing hospitality; but it's just not my gift.

However, I have taught English to a classroom of 30 adults from other countries, including some that did not speak any language that I know. I have taught Bible classes, Spanish and sign language as well. Teaching is my gift. As long as I can feed people information instead of food, I do well. Once I stopped trying to imitate my mother and started using the gifts God gave me, I relaxed and became more confident. Over time I have realised that we each have unique abilities that we can use to serve God and others.

Prayer: *Dear Lord, help us to recognise the special abilities that you have instilled in us and to use them in service to you. Amen*

Thought for the day: We all have special gifts from God.

Mary Hunt Webb (New Mexico, US)

Overwhelming love

Read Psalm 103:1–12

We love because God first loved us.
1 John 4:19 (CEB)

I was ready for bed when Keri, my two-year-old granddaughter, came bouncing in. She was returning from a day at the lake, where she had been visiting her paternal grandmother. She jumped in my lap and we exchanged hugs and kisses. The next instant she was still and snuggled in my arms. I held her, thinking of how much I love her. Watching all this, my daughter said, 'Mum, she's filthy! Why are you letting her sit on your lap?' I had to admit that the scent of dirt, puppies, fish, food, lake and a lot of running around radiated from her little body. Somehow, it didn't matter to me. She didn't need to be clean for me to love her. She didn't need to be perfect. In fact, nothing she could do would make me love her any more or any less. I would do anything for her. The love I felt at that moment was overwhelming.

As I held her, the word filthy reminded me of Isaiah 64:6: 'All of us have become like one who is unclean, and all our righteous acts are like filthy rags' (NIV). As I thought about the verse, God flooded my soul with a new understanding. The unconditional love I felt for my granddaughter was like the unconditional love my heavenly Father had for me. I, like Keri, go to God imperfect and, like Keri, I find love.

Prayer: *Dear God, give us a deeper understanding of your unconditional love, and help us to extend love to others. Amen*

Thought for the day: To whom can I show God's unconditional love today?

Marsha Howard (Texas, US)

PRAYER FOCUS: THOSE WHO DON'T FEEL GOD'S LOVE

In the fire

Read Daniel 3:13–28

[Nebuchadnezzar] replied, 'But I see four men unbound, walking in the middle of the fire, and they are not hurt; and the fourth has the appearance of a god.'
Daniel 3:25 (NRSV)

When I was young, I used to go and visit my grandmother, who was a potter. She would let me pick out a ceramic piece to paint. When I had finished painting, my grandmother would put the piece into the incredibly hot kiln, then take it out and put a protective glaze on it before firing it again. This glaze would bring out the colour, making the creation shiny and more durable. The ceramic pieces always looked more brilliant after having gone through the firing process.

When Shadrach, Meshach and Abednego were thrown into a fire for being faithful to God by refusing to worship Nebuchadnezzar's golden statue, they had no certainty that God would save them. Yet, while peering into the flames, the king was astonished that they appeared to be unharmed, and with them was a fourth person who had a divine appearance.

Intense suffering can leave its mark on us. God does not promise to keep us from the fiery furnace, but he is with us in it. And like a ceramic piece that becomes even more beautiful after having been through the kiln, God can take the most intense moments in our lives and form us into something different, too – something more beautiful, more durable and more like Christ.

Prayer: *Dear Lord, in moments of suffering, grant us peace as we seek to be transformed into the likeness of your Son, Jesus Christ. Amen*

Thought for the day: God does not promise to keep me from the fire but to be with me in it.

Adam Benson (North Carolina, US)

My hiding place

Read Luke 6:12–16

You are my hiding place; you will protect me from trouble and surround me with songs of deliverance.
Psalm 32:7 (NIV)

A few years ago, I was struggling with several problems. I didn't know what to do and had no one to talk to. I decided to seek a quiet place so I could take all my concerns to God. I chose a small room on the second floor of my home. There I sat down and began to pray. I talked with God about all that had happened and asked for wisdom and guidance. My heart had been filled with fear and worry, but in that room I felt calm as God's presence filled my heart. I knew that my Lord would never leave me alone.

That room is still my quiet place. There I pray, read the Bible and sometimes sing aloud to God. Although my quiet room is special to me, being in God's presence is more than special to me. He is truly my hiding place. And in every situation or circumstance I face, whether happy or sad, I can find refuge in his presence.

Prayer: *Dear God, whatever happens in our lives, you are our hope and our strength. We do not need to be afraid, for in you we can find rest for our souls. We pray as Jesus taught us, saying, 'Our Father which art in heaven, Hallowed be thy name. Thy kingdom come. Thy will be done, as in heaven, so in earth. Give us day by day our daily bread. And forgive us our sins; for we also forgive every one that is indebted to us. And lead us not into temptation; but deliver us from evil.'* Amen*

Thought for the day: Whatever happens, God is my hiding place.

Meliana Santoso (East Java, Indonesia)

PRAYER FOCUS: THOSE WHO ARE IN DANGER

*Luke 11:2–4, KJV

Peace in the storm

Read Luke 8:22–25

Then they cried out to the Lord in their trouble, and he brought them out of their distress. He stilled the storm to a whisper; the waves of the sea were hushed.
Psalm 107:28–29 (NIV)

How would you have acted in that boat with Jesus? Many years ago I was crossing the Irish Sea in a passenger boat without stabilisers in bad weather. When those angry, huge dark waves seemed to rise above our heads I was sure the boat would sink and, yes, I was very afraid. Tables tilted, chairs slid across the deck and crockery smashed to the floor, ignored by the staff who held on to doorframes to keep upright. Fortunately the crossing only lasted a couple of hours and when on dry land again I felt rather ashamed of my cowardice. Based on that experience I'm sure I would have panicked in the same way as the disciples did on their little boat.

Years later I went through another 'storm', a bad patch that seemed to last forever, and there was nothing I could do to change it. I could only find peace by handing the situation over to God. And eventually the storm passed.

It's so easy to forget God's presence when the storms of life are raging. I have to remember to pray about my fears, and to have faith in his power and judgement to still the storm in the way that Jesus did for the disciples.

Prayer: *Father God, thank you that you are always there for us in any storm. Help us to call upon you when we face trouble and to trust that you will help us. Amen*

Thought for the day: God will always hear our prayers.

Edna Hutchings (Dorset, England)

Paul's prayer

Read Luke 11:1–10

We have not ceased praying for you and asking that you may be filled with the knowledge of God's will in all spiritual wisdom and understanding, so that you may lead lives worthy of the Lord.
Colossians 1:9–10 (NRSV)

When I visited my daughter Tonya recently, she showed me the cards that she hands out to strangers as she travels. They say, 'I Said a Prayer for You Today'. I was so impressed! She gave me several and I began to do the same thing. I was pleased by the first reaction I got. The receptionist at the doctor's surgery said, 'Thank you. I was having a difficult day today. I will keep this card next to me.'

My experience led me to consider how I actually pray for others. Paul tells us that he was praying for the church members at Colossae even though he had never met them. What was he praying? He tells us that he was praying that these strangers would first be filled with the knowledge of God's will for their lives and that they would 'lead lives worthy of the Lord'.

We all need prayer. We can always ask how we can pray for others if they have specific needs like finding a new job, helping a lost son or daughter or improving their health. But when we are not sure what to pray for others, we can remember Paul's prayer for the people in Colossae.

Prayer: *Our Father, thank you for hearing our prayers for those who are hurting today. In Jesus' name, we ask you to be with them and that they will be aware of your presence. Amen*

Thought for the day: For whom will I pray today?

David Jones (Georgia, US)

The man who had everything

Read 1 John 1:8—2:2

[David] said, 'I will confess my transgressions to the Lord.' And you forgave the guilt of my sin.
Psalm 32:5 (NIV)

Looking around the table at the other Bible study participants, I wondered what had drawn each of them to this 13-week study of King David. Some were leaders like David. A couple of people were exceptional musicians like David. I wondered if any of them wrote poetry, as David had.

I marvelled inwardly at how very gifted King David had been and wished that God had favoured me with such outstanding talents and attributes. I was sure I had nothing in common with him. By the end of the study, however, my perspective had shifted. I had learned that, despite his talents and leadership skills, David sometimes made bad decisions, as we all do. Yet King David also had the humility and integrity to recognise his sin, take responsibility for it and accept its sometimes devastating consequences. In the aftermath of terrible losses and trials, he chose the righteous path of praising God and requesting his guidance every step of the way forward.

To my surprise, that Bible study revealed how much I have in common with David. Like his, my life is an occasionally painful journey made ultimately triumphant when I lean on God's faithful promises to guide and redeem my life.

Prayer: *Holy God, remind us not to compare ourselves to others but instead to focus on our unique relationship with you. Amen*

Thought for the day: Despite my imperfections, God loves me generously.

Prudence Schofield (Maine, US)

The way

Read John 14:1–14

Jesus answered, 'I am the way and the truth and the life.'
John 14:6 (NIV)

Only weeks after arriving in England to work, my wife and I set out to drive across London. Struggling to keep to the correct lane, we suddenly found ourselves on a very large roundabout with several lanes of traffic. Signs confused us and we could not identify the road for our destination. Changing lanes seemed fraught with danger. We decided to stay in our lane and made a complete circuit. On the second time around, the signs began to make sense and we identified our exit as well as how to change lanes. Soon we were safely on our way.

Often, grief, setbacks or radically changed circumstances leave us uncertain and confused. We circle – in a crisis of indecision and sometimes of faith. We question which way will lead us onward and upward. The first crucial step is to believe that there is a way and then, in faith and prayer, to see it.

Christians know that Christ is the way. When we look to him and see that he responded to anger with love; accepted those rejecting him; demonstrated loyalty, strength and gentleness; and lived by faith in his heavenly Father, we can follow him as the way for all of us.

Prayer: *Dear Lord Jesus, help us to seek your way every day. Amen*

Thought for the day: Jesus assures me that there is a way forward.

Everard Blackman (Queensland, Australia)

The true source of comfort

Read Job 1:18–22

[God] comforts us in all our troubles, so that we can comfort those in any trouble with the comfort we ourselves receive from God.
2 Corinthians 1:4 (NIV)

The death of my two-year-old granddaughter followed by the death of my only child 23 months later left me in a wilderness of grief that had my soul searching for answers. Why? Why them? Why me? How do I survive this? What do you want from me, God?

I searched for answers to those questions during that painful time in my life. Everything and everyone around me offered only temporary relief from my grief. In my greatest suffering I realised that God was my only true source of comfort. The Holy Spirit comforted me and gave me a peace beyond understanding. This comfort did not take the pain away suddenly or shorten my time of grief. Instead it shifted my focus from the circumstances to the Saviour, Jesus Christ.

We all experience painful circumstances that cause us to despair. But God is with us even in the most tragic situations. He comforts us and empowers us to comfort others with the comfort we have received.

Prayer: *Dear Father, thank you for being with us during our deepest grief. Help us to trust you through the pain. Amen*

Thought for the day: God is present even in my deepest grief.

Princess Miller (Texas, US)

God's works of art

Read Ephesians 2:8–10

We are God's handiwork, created in Christ Jesus to do good works, which God prepared in advance for us to do.
Ephesians 2:10 (NIV)

Our youngest daughter is a gifted quilter. After hearing me speak about these verses in Ephesians, she said to me, with a smile, that a quilt is a useful work of art. As I thought about how quilts are made and used, I realised that she was right. Depending on the quilt's intended purpose, the quilter chooses the fabrics, pattern, size and the intricacy of the design. Although many quilts are created to be objects of beauty – and we have several of our daughter's quilts displayed in our home – most are made to be used. We have one spread across our bed, and we have some smaller ones that we use to keep warm in during chilly winter evenings.

Just as a master quilter carefully constructs quilts, so our God has created us specifically for the good works that our particular skills, talents and gifts can meet. God has stitched us in love and graced us with faith; it is our responsibility to follow his way for us and reach out to those he brings across our path. We are to serve God as useful works of art.

Prayer: *Thank you, God, for creating us as your works of art. Help us to use our gifts and talents to surround others with your love. Amen*

Thought for the day: God created me to be a useful work of art.

Sara Powell (Georgia, US)

The hope of refuge

Read Matthew 2:13–15

I was hungry and you gave me food to eat. I was thirsty and you gave me a drink. I was a stranger and you welcomed me.
Matthew 25:35 (CEB)

We have many refugees in our world today. Some flee civil war or violence. Others have seen their homes destroyed by natural disaster or the infrastructure and industry of their community devastated. The number of refugees saddens many of us, especially because refugees are not always welcomed with open arms.

In the Bible we read about one refugee family in particular – Mary, Joseph and the baby Jesus. If they had not fled their country seeking refuge, the baby would have been killed by King Herod's order. Many present-day refugees also face certain death if they remain in their own country. Even when they leave, the danger is not over. They face a perilous journey to other lands.

Mary and Joseph were able to return to their homeland after Herod died and the danger had passed. Many of today's refugees hope for the same result: they dream of when they might return home once again.

With refugees, those of us who have not been displaced can hope and pray for peace that will allow them to return to their homelands. While we pray, we can also heed Christ's call to welcome the stranger. As Christians we are called to do all we can for the refugees on our own doorstep.

Prayer: *God of peace, keep us ever mindful of Jesus' teachings and that when we care for others, we honour him. Amen*

Thought for the day: How open are my arms to God's people seeking refuge?

Bill Findlay (Glasgow, Scotland)

True love

Read Mark 8:31–36

*We know love by this, that [the Son of God] laid down his life for us –
and we ought to lay down our lives for one another.*
1 John 3:16 (NRSV)

Early in our marriage, my husband proclaimed that he would be willing
to die for me. I thought my husband's dramatic declaration sounded
good, but I didn't completely believe him. The evening before, when
we were out for dinner, Michael had a milkshake. I didn't want a whole
milkshake – just a few sips. I had a sip of his, then another and another.
Michael said, 'Why don't you order your own milkshake?' So I challenged him: 'You would die for me, but you don't want to share your
milkshake?'

We now laugh about the Milkshake Incident. We have learned that to
love each other as Christ loves us doesn't mean making a big, dramatic
gesture. It means making countless small sacrifices for each other.

Michael shows me that he loves me when he speaks kindly to me
when I am in a bad mood. He works hard to support our family and
does chores around the house when he'd rather do something else. He
rubs my feet when they hurt. He even freely shares his milkshakes with
me. His daily actions show me that he is laying down his life for me.

Most of us won't have to die to show our love for others. But we can
let go of our own desires in order to love and serve the people in our
lives, as a small reflection of what Jesus did in giving up everything
for us.

Prayer: *Dear Father, may the example of Jesus' selfless love inspire us
to lay down our own lives in love as well. Amen*

Thought for the day: How will I reflect Christ's self-sacrificing love to
others?

Kristi Iachetta (Texas, US)

Trust in the Lord

Read Deuteronomy 31:1–8

In you our ancestors put their trust; they trusted and you delivered them.
Psalm 22:4 (NIV)

I love stories with happy endings – in which all the problems are solved, all the loose ends tied up and all the people live happily ever after. I've had some happy endings in my life but I've also endured sadness caused by the loss of jobs, possessions and loved ones. Through the years, I've discovered that life is more like an adventure than a fairytale.

Moses had his ups and downs, too. He grew up in luxury, committed a crime, fled to another country, found a wife and had a family. Then he came back to his homeland to lead a grumbling nation through the wilderness and died before entering the Promised Land. Throughout his journey, Moses experienced both honour and hardship. He followed, trusted and obeyed God. And he faced his trials with great courage.

In the adventure of life, the road is often rough, with challenges around every corner, and happy endings are not guaranteed. Currently, I'm struggling with a health issue and have no idea what will happen. But if I follow the example of Moses, I know that God will be present with me. If we follow Moses' advice to Joshua to be of great courage because God is with us, we can find the strength to endure hardships. If we choose to trust and obey, like Moses and Joshua, we will find that our trust in God's faithfulness is well placed.

Prayer: *Dear Father, help us to trust in your faithful promise to be with us whatever life brings. Amen*

Thought for the day: In whatever life brings, I can trust God's faithfulness.

Lynn Karidis (Michigan, US)

A rebuilding project

Read Matthew 5:14–16

Let your light shine before others, that they may see your good deeds and glorify your Father in heaven.
Matthew 5:16 (NIV)

Our community had been ravaged by terrible flooding. Many houses owned by the elderly and lower income families were severely damaged. Churches in our community started an 'adopt a house' scheme, by which they would cover the expense of all the supplies and labour needed to gut and restore an 'adopted' house. I organised this project at our church but I had no idea how it would turn out.

Members of all ages volunteered their time and money. Many brought friends and neighbours to help. When I went to buy supplies for the project, most builders' merchants either donated the materials or supplied them at cost. Strangers in the community who saw us working often joined in to help. The project became a tremendous success. Phyllis, the owner of the house I worked on, shed tears of joy.

God will surely give us all opportunities to be Christ's hands and feet. Sometimes those opportunities may seem daunting. But if we trust God, our light can shine brighter than we could have ever imagined.

Prayer: *Dear God, give us the courage to shine our light in this world so that others can see you clearly. Amen*

Thought for the day: Where can I shine God's light for others today?

Lou Eppelsheimer, Jr (Arizona, US)

Relationship with God

Read Luke 10:38–42

Be not conformed to this world: but be ye transformed by the renewing of your mind, that ye may prove what is that good, and acceptable, and perfect, will of God.
Romans 12:2 (KJV)

A few years ago, I was so busy looking after home and family, attending church meetings and helping people in need, that I ended up leaving aside the most important thing: nurturing my relationship with God. This didn't happen because I had forgotten God. On the contrary, I could not get through the day without him. I prayed unceasingly for several people and for my relationship with him out of habit. But I was so distracted by the many tasks I had to do that I did not spend enough time alone with God to feel connected and renewed.

In today's reading, Martha had no time to be with the Lord, for she was 'worried and distracted by many things', forgetting 'the better part' (CEB). I felt upset by the thought that I was acting like Martha.

At any given time, we can be busy with many things that we believe will please God. However, in reality, we may be neglecting what is essential to keeping us closer to him and doing his will. It is important that as we are seeking to serve the Lord, we also devote our lives to prayer and Bible study to help us to know God better and to discern the best role for us in his kingdom.

Prayer: *Merciful God, help us to choose the better part which you have prepared in order to nourish our relationship with you. Amen*

Thought for the day: Spending time alone with God equips me to serve others.

Leopoldina João Pedro (Luanda, Angola)

Wild turkey feathers

Each day I go for a walk around the university campus near my office. I enjoy being outside, seeing whatever there is to see – the leaves changing colours, the blue sky, a squirrel with an acorn in its mouth. Walking helps clear my mind and it keeps me close to God by keeping me close to his creation.

Since I tend to be something of a worrier, a walk eases the spinning of my mind about the concerns of the day. On some days the concerns are small. On others, worries overtake me. With each passing year, I feel less invincible and protected than I did the year before. With age has come the sense that I am not as immune to difficulties, challenges and loss as I once thought.

It's easy to dwell on all that could go wrong. It's easy to worry about bad news we have received or bad news we fear we might receive. It's easy to worry about the future and how we will deal with it when it gets here. It's easy to become so paralysed by fear that we can barely get through the day.

There are turkeys living in the woods surrounding my house and in one sense they have helped to reduce my worry. I see them from my kitchen window as they move through my garden, pecking insects from the ground. When I walk on the land I share with these magnificent birds, I often find a discarded feather or two. When I see one, I pick it up, take it back to the house with me and put it in an old brass pot that sits in my fireplace. I do not remember when or why I started collecting the feathers, only that it seems to me a pity to leave something so beautiful lying on the ground.

Over time, my brass pot full of feathers has come to symbolise the elegance and simplicity that surround me each day. Contemplating my feathers helps me to clear my head and reminds me that the God of creation cares about me and watches over me. The God who created the turkeys, their feathers, the ground they fall upon and each of us,

69

can handle anything that I'm faced with. I appreciate what Job – a man who certainly had many concerns – says about this: 'But ask the animals, and they will teach you; the birds of the air, and they will tell you; ask the plants of the earth, and they will teach you; and the fish of the sea will declare to you. Who… does not know that the hand of the Lord has done this? In his hand is the life of every living thing' (Job 12:7–10, NRSV). Job's trust in God is astounding, especially considering all that he had gone through and everything that he must have been thinking.

My turkey feathers are wonders that continue to teach me to stop and look around at all the other wonders of my life day in and day out. They are not flashy but small miracles that God sets in my path each day for me to notice and reflect on. The feathers remind me to stop obsessing about all that could go wrong and focus instead on all that is going right.

A squirrel with an acorn and a wild turkey feather are just two of the many daily reminders of the wonder around me. When the day gets hard, I try to stop and look around at all of God's miracles in creation. When I do, I remember that 'in his hand is the life of every living thing' (Job 12:10). And this is enough to help me get through almost any day.

Several meditations in this issue address worry and small wonders. You may want to read again the meditations for September 3, 4, 9, 10, 17, 20, 25, October 2 and 14, November 12 and 27, and December 15, 17 and 24 before responding to the reflection questions below.

Questions for reflection

1 When have you worried about something in your life that never came to pass? What were your prayers like during this time? What did this experience teach you about worrying?

2 Where do you feel closest to God? Why do you feel closest to him there?

3 Name some small ways that you could take time each day to grow closer to God. Which of these appeals to you most?

Andrew Garland Breeden
Associate Editor, Acquisitions

Being what I am

Read Luke 10:25–37

You have taken off your old self with its practices and have put on the new self, which is being renewed in knowledge in the image of its Creator.

Colossians 3:9–10 (NIV)

'I am who I am' (Exodus 3:14), the Lord replied when Moses asked his name. And then I thought of my usual response when people ask who I am. I might tell them my name or that I'm an artist or a writer, but none of these labels would matter if I were not truly who I say I am. Saying I'm a teacher would be meaningless if I don't truly teach and pass on knowledge.

In the same way, saying that I am a Christian won't matter if I don't display Christlike behaviour or show love to my neighbours. In today's reading, the priest and the Levite were men of God, but the Samaritan – viewed as an outcast and idol worshipper – showed more compassion to the wounded stranger than they did. In this, the Samaritan showed that he wasn't his stereotype or title but simply a man capable of showing compassion and love to a total stranger, to his neighbour. Jesus' answer to the lawyer showed us that our titles and labels do not matter much. In the end it is not about saying who we are – Levite, priest, Samaritan, friend, mother or writer. What matters is showing who we really are – children of God, striving to be conformed to the image of our Creator.

Prayer: *Dear Lord, help us to love you with all our heart and soul and strength and mind, and to love our fellow human beings as ourselves. Amen*

Thought for the day: Today I will be my true self – a child of God.

Uyo Ani (Ukraine)

A family for everyone

Read Isaiah 46:3–4

God sets the lonely in families, he leads out the prisoners with singing.
Psalm 68:6 (NIV)

I have Asperger's syndrome, a form of autism that makes social interactions difficult. My condition would make it hard for me to support a wife and family in the way I would want to. As a result, I decided it was best that I remain single. But one concern that used to keep me up at night was: 'Who will take care of me when I am old and can no longer care for myself?'

One day I was encouraged when I came across the psalm quoted above. Families do not have to be related by blood but can be united by a common goal, as with the body of Christ. We can't always rely even on blood relations, but we can depend on our family who is united in Christ.

This verse assures us that God provides us with support through friends and, more importantly, a church family. In the course of his ministry, Paul, who was single, often expressed gratitude for the ways that different church members provided for his needs at all stages of his life.

Prayer: *Compassionate God, thank you for giving us the opportunity to belong to a kind and loving family. Amen*

Thought for the day: As a Christian, I am part of the family of Christ.

Aaron Tanner (Alabama, US)

Hoping for a miracle

Read Philippians 4:4–9

The peace of God, which transcends all understanding, will guard your hearts and your minds in Christ Jesus.

Philippians 4:7 (NIV)

For 36 hours, I had watched helplessly while my newborn daughter fought for her life. In a coma, Amee needed machines to breathe for her, monitor her heart and supply her with nourishment and medication. Her chance of survival stood at five per cent. My anxious thoughts became jumbled prayers. As I began to wonder if my prayers reached beyond the ceiling, God began to fill my heart with the words from Paul quoted above.

I gave my doubts, anxieties and fears to God. As I gave him thanks for the gift of my daughter, I realised that God loved her more than I ever could. As soon as I sincerely uttered the words, 'I trust you, God, to heal my daughter in your way and your timing,' I felt peace as if a warm blanket were wrapped around me. My baby's situation had not changed, but my attitude had.

Throughout these past 34 years of Amee's life, I have seen medical impossibilities become reality and have continued to praise God for this unfolding miracle. When we turn over to God all the circumstances of our lives, he can take our jumbled prayers and do more than we could ever ask or imagine. The answers, the miracles, might not be what we expected – but they just might be exactly what we need.

Prayer: *Heavenly Father, help us to trust you in all the circumstances of our lives. Amen*

Thought for the day: God knows exactly what I need.

Carol Harrison (Saskatchewan, Canada)

Despite mistakes

Read Exodus 3:7–15

Moses said to God, 'Who am I that I should go to Pharaoh, and bring the Israelites out of Egypt?'
Exodus 3:11 (NRSV)

A friend of mine bought a house to renovate. When he had rebuilt the walls, I came in to paint the rooms. The first thing I had to do was to put filler in all the cracks. Since Dan knew how many cracks he had left, he was impressed with how the job looked after I smoothed the filler into place – and even more excited after he saw each painted wall.

At one point I was halfway through my work on a wall when I took a break to rest my back. Because many of the cracks were not yet filled, I thought, 'I hope Dan doesn't walk in now; he'd probably fire me!' Then I thought about my own life: recently divorced, too many credit cards used to their limit, a bankruptcy in my past. God should fire me too.

Then I remembered that God didn't fire Moses, even after he had killed a man. In fact, one day God chose Moses to lead the children of Israel to the Promised Land. He used Moses, a murderer, for divine work – and he can use each of us too.

Our past mistakes don't have to prevent us from serving God. The future has yet to be written, and he can call any one of us to accomplish divine work.

Prayer: *Dear heavenly Father, thank you for calling us to divine work despite our mistakes. Use us to build your kingdom for Jesus' sake. Amen*

Thought for the day: God gives second chances.

Wade Webster (Texas, US)

The secret

Read Philippians 4:10–13

I have learned the secret of being content in any and every situation.
Philippians 4:12 (NIV)

Years ago, my job required me to move halfway across the country. For the first few months I felt very content. I had a good job, a nice apartment near the beach and a close friend for a roommate. Then a couple of friends from home came to visit and questioned how I could be happy there. They pointed out that I was many miles from home, did not have a lot of friends and not much of a social life. 'Don't you feel isolated and miss home?' they asked. From that point on, I did feel isolated and lonely and eventually moved back home.

Later, I realised that their comments had shifted my focus from what I had to what I was missing. I now understand that, in many situations, our contentment depends on how we perceive and value our circumstances.

Certainly this is true in the context of Paul's writing in Philippians 4. Paul's circumstances at that time were dire. Yet in spite of all kinds of hardships, he 'learned the secret of being content'. He goes on to reveal his secret: 'I can do all things through [Christ] who strengthens me' (NRSV). The secret to my contentment is found in Jesus Christ. So we can focus our attention not on what might be missing in our lives but rather on all the blessings that God has lavished on us.

Prayer: *Dear God, help us to focus on the blessings you give us and to recognise that we draw our strength through your Son and our Saviour, Jesus Christ. Amen*

Thought for the day: What blessing from God have I been overlooking?

Scott Martin (New Jersey, US)

Delivered

Read Psalm 34:1–9

I sought the Lord, and he heard me, and delivered me from all my fears.
Psalm 34:4 (KJV)

It was 2 o'clock in the morning, and I sat by my bedside, sweating profusely and wondering how I'd managed to escape. I had just awakened from yet another terrible dream, this time featuring a large python that was pursuing me and about to swallow me. I added this to my list of fears and wondered if I could really be delivered from all my fears in the way that King David was in the verse quoted above. But instead I prayed and a few minutes later I felt safe and fearless through Christ.

Life can be full of fearsome encounters – the fear of not being able to continue paying for a place to live, the fear of all things falling apart in a relationship you've devoted yourself to, the fear of having nightmares each time you go to sleep. But in his psalms, David teaches us that when we seek God, we will be delivered from all kinds of fears.

Prayer: *Thank you, Lord, for delivering us from all our fears. We pray as Jesus taught us, saying, 'Our Father which art in heaven, Hallowed be thy name. Thy kingdom come. Thy will be done in earth, as it is in heaven. Give us this day our daily bread. And forgive us our debts, as we forgive our debtors. And lead us not into temptation, but deliver us from evil: For thine is the kingdom, and the power, and the glory, for ever. Amen.'**

Thought for the day: Today when my fears arise, I will remember that God will give me peace.

Vimbai Chizarura (Zimbabwe)

PRAYER FOCUS: THOSE SUFFERING FROM RECURRENT NIGHTMARES
*Matthew 6:9–13, KJV

No one is insignificant

Read Joshua 1:1–9

Be strong and courageous. Do not be afraid; do not be discouraged, for the Lord your God will be with you wherever you go.
Joshua 1:9 (NIV)

I had recently arrived in the United States and didn't know anyone. For a year, I worked for a telephone marketing company in a low-paying job, and it was difficult for me to make ends meet. I hoped that this job would be temporary because talking daily on the telephone to customers who insulted me made me feel insignificant and distressed.

Then one evening while I was making a routine call, the woman who answered the phone was crying and pleaded with me to call the emergency services. She had been attacked in a situation of domestic violence. Immediately, I dialled the right number and gave the woman's details to the operator. I left my desk to take a few moments to compose myself and began to pray for God's strength for the woman and her situation.

In that moment, I realised that God can use each of us wherever we are. Because I was at my 'insignificant' job, a woman in need was helped. I learned that no person is unimportant when we serve God by helping a neighbour – or a stranger.

Prayer: *Merciful God, continue to shine your light on us as we seek to do your will and to help those in need. In the name of Christ. Amen*

Thought for the day: No one is insignificant in God's eyes.

Zully Taborda (New York, US)

Giving with joy

Read Malachi 3:6–10

Bring the full tithe into the storehouse… says the Lord of hosts; see if I will not open the windows of heaven for you and pour down for you an overflowing blessing.
Malachi 3:10 (NRSV)

Until 2008 my wife and I had not tithed regularly. Our resources were already insufficient to support most of our needs. We were afraid that if we gave regularly, we would not have enough left to live on.

One day, as we reflected on today's reading from Malachi, we realised that we needed to tithe. We felt obligated to renew our commitment to the maintenance of our local church life. Later our resources began to increase, and we understood that tithing was an expression of our recognition that God is the Creator and that all we have belongs to him.

Acts 20:35 reminds us, 'It is more blessed to give than to receive' (NIV). Tithing and other offerings can be joyful acts of love. And the blessings we receive from God are greater than what we contribute to the harvest.

Prayer: *Eternal God, teach us to contribute sincerely and regularly to your work in the world. Amen*

Thought for the day: What gifts can I offer to God today?

Aguinaldo Agostinho (Luanda, Angola)

The carer's carer

Read Isaiah 40:27–31

He gives strength to the weary and increases the power of the weak.
Isaiah 40:29 (NIV)

For six years, I was the carer for my husband who was suffering from early-onset Alzheimer's disease. During that time, I faced many challenges. He is now in a nursing home, but many times during those years I felt like a prisoner in my own home and wanted to give up. Totally frustrated, I would ask myself, 'Why can't he do this simple task?' or 'Why is he getting so agitated over a television programme?' Then I had to tell myself, 'He cannot help himself; it is the disease.'

Things were changing; his world was turning upside down and that was frightening for him. As my husband declined more and more each day, I prayed for God to give me the patience and strength to care for him with love and dignity. At times I did not know how I was going to make it, but God stepped in and gave me the strength, patience and understanding I needed to view my husband as separate from the disease.

Whenever we think that we cannot go any further or do not know how we are going to cope with a tough situation, we can remember that God is always there to see us through it. As we pray and meditate on his word, we feel that presence more and more. The problem may not go away, but God will help us deal with it.

Prayer: *Dear Lord, give us the strength and patience to lean on you in the midst of our problems. Amen*

Thought for the day: God will give me strength to love and care for those around me.

Joyce Irvin (New York, US)

Dream big

Read Genesis 18:1–15

Everything is possible for one who believes.
Mark 9:23 (NIV)

In 2015, when I told my friend Andrey that I often sent my devotional writing to *The Upper Room*, he said, 'Linawati, I am waiting for you to publish your first book.' I thought he was kidding me, but he wasn't. Encouraged by his words, I started to write a Christian book and when I finally finished it I sent it to a publisher.

The publisher rejected my work but I decided not to give up. I sent it to another publisher and finally, in December 2016, my book was published.

At first, writing a book seemed like too big a dream. While I was waiting for an answer from the second publisher, I remember asking myself, 'Am I talented enough? Am I dreaming too big?'

When God shows us something seemingly impossible we are to do, like Sarah we may laugh and say to ourselves, 'Stop hoping for it. You can't realise such a dream.' But we can remember that nothing is impossible for God. The apostle Paul wrote to the Philippians, 'I can do all things through [God] who strengthens me' (Philippians 4:13, NRSV). And so can we.

Prayer: *Thank you, God, that with you we can follow our dreams – because we know that for you, nothing is impossible. Amen*

Thought for the day: What seems impossible for me is very possible for God.

Linawati Santoso (East Java, Indonesia)

A week of summer

Read Philippians 2:1–7

Do nothing from selfish ambition or conceit, but in humility regard others as better than yourselves.
Philippians 2:3 (NRSV)

Just a few weeks into my summer break, I saw the months ahead as full of the promise of fun and relaxation. I was ready to enjoy every day. But my mum had a different plan. Without my consent, she signed me up to help children during a week-long Holiday Bible Club. My first reaction was frustration and anger. I felt that my precious summer had been spoiled and my plans ruined – at least for a whole week. I argued for a while, but nothing changed.

When the week arrived, I woke up early and went to my church unhappy and full of dread. All I could think of was how I could have slept in much later, and all the other things I could be doing. But my attitude soon changed. From the moment I met the children, I realised that I was there for a greater purpose. As I saw them singing about God's wonders and completing Bible activities, I knew that God was using me and my gifts to serve children on their faith journey.

Paul's words in Philippians 2:1–7 helped me to see that if I had acted selfishly, I would not have made any positive impact on the Christian community. However, because I had carried out my assignment as a servant of God, I was able to influence the lives of the children around me. In turn, I could think of no better way to spend a week of my summer.

Prayer: *Dear God, help us to be grateful for our many blessings and gifts and to use them to help others. Amen*

Thought for the day: I will use what God has given me to serve others.

Matthew Hammes (North Carolina, US)

Open my eyes

Read 1 Samuel 16:1–13

The Lord said to Samuel, 'Do not consider his appearance or his height… The Lord does not look at the things people look at. People look at the outward appearance, but the Lord looks at the heart.'
1 Samuel 16:7 (NIV)

On a recent camping trip, I spent some time staring at the stars. At first a light cloud layer made it difficult to see them, but the clouds soon melted away, leaving a clear panorama with millions of twinkling stars. Living in the city, I'm not used to seeing such a vast array. I noticed that the longer I stared, the more stars became visible. It was as if the beauty was multiplying before my eyes, revealing stars that had been obscured by the glow of lights from the city.

Unfortunately, sometimes I allow stereotypes or the busyness of this world to obscure the beauty of those around me. I don't look long enough for their true worth to come into focus. In today's reading, Samuel assumed that God would choose Eliab as his anointed. Yet eventually, Samuel was reminded that God does not look at things as humans do. We see only the surface, but God knows a person's heart and sees their true worth. God saw in David, his anointed, qualities that those around him had been unable to see.

Rather than focusing just on the surface, I want to be the kind of person who sees the qualities of someone's heart and the value of every person.

Prayer: *Dear Lord, help us to look past stereotypes and see those around us through your eyes. Amen*

Thought for the day: Each day, I will open my eyes to see others the way God sees them.

Victoria Kubasak (California, US)

Words that matter

Read John 4:1–26, 39–42

Many of the Samaritans from that town believed in [Jesus] because of the woman's testimony, 'He told me everything I've ever done.'
John 4:39 (NIV)

One day, a young couple knocked at my door. I had no idea who they were or why they had come until the woman said, 'You once spoke to me of things that mattered when I was a rebellious teenager.' She said that the words I had used had rung in her ears and heart to the extent that they changed her life. As a result, she left her wild friends behind and went to college, and accepted Jesus as her personal Saviour. Now she is happily married.

She ended with, 'I came to say thank you.'

This woman's words reminded me of what the Samaritan woman said about Jesus, that he had told her everything about her life. This experience became a turning point in her life. She went out to tell the villagers, and many people believed. If we are mindful of the words that we speak, they can help lead others to God.

Prayer: *Dear Lord Jesus, help us to speak words that are full of your love, truth and hope. Amen*

Thought for the day: Today I will share God's love through words of encouragement.

Charlotte Mande Ilunga (Western Cape, South Africa)

To be patient

Read 2 Peter 1:3–11

Be patient with everyone.
1 Thessalonians 5:14 (NIV)

My husband's dirty overalls were left on the bedroom floor– again. I was trying to calm down and remember all his good traits. I'm sure he gets upset with me over minor things too. He and I have been married for 47 years. That's a long time to be with someone.

One day I read the verse above with Paul's final advice to the Thessalonians, 'Be patient with everyone.' The next time I saw the overalls, I said to myself, 'Every time I wake up to overalls on the floor, I'm going to start thanking God for some little thing my husband does right.' Before I knew it, I'd found so much to be thankful for that now I praise God for those overalls! I often thank God for giving me my husband to share my life. I also make sure to tell him how much he means to me.

I've decided to do that same thing with people who irritate me. Instead of focusing on the negative, I think of some good thing about them and praise God for that. Maybe if we all become inspired to pay attention to what Paul wrote, gradually this world will become more patient and loving!

Prayer: *Kind and loving God, help us to be patient with everyone we meet today. In Jesus' name, we pray. Amen*

Thought for the day: Today, I will turn my irritation into praise.

Nancy R. Meyer (Nebraska, US)

Hearing God's voice

Read John 10:1–6

[The Lord] has shown you, O mortal, what is good. And what does the Lord require of you? To act justly and to love mercy and to walk humbly with your God.
Micah 6:8 (NIV)

As a swimming coach for people with special needs, I have the privilege of working with swimmers of all ages. Without question I receive more than I give from this experience, which has spanned over ten years. Our swimmers have gone on to compete at national and international levels – often winning their events.

Recently I was helping a swimmer who is blind prepare for competition. We tried a number of ways to assist her, but the best was to have a coach get ahead of her in the pool and talk to her. She could hear his voice and swim in that direction, allowing her to learn and then finally successfully compete. Because she could not see the wall of the pool, in competition we extended a tennis ball on a long pole to alert her that she was approaching the wall so that she would not hit her head as she finished.

God also walks in front of me and gives me direction. While I am not always aware of it, I do know that he is present and caring. When I can hear God's voice I progress more rapidly, feel better about myself and accomplish more. Sometimes I miss the 'tennis ball on a stick' and crash into walls. Even then, however, I am uplifted by the knowledge that God will be with me when I try again.

Prayer: *Dear God, thank you for walking in front of us and showing us the way. And, when we fail, thanks for staying with us as we try again. Amen*

Thought for the day: Today I will listen for God's guidance.

John Cruden (Virginia, US)

God's word

Read Psalm 119:9–16
I have hidden your word in my heart.
Psalm 119:11 (NIV)

A friend told me that he never left the house without his keys, his phone and his Bible. All three were essential bits of equipment to him.

I have a mobile phone and I carry it with me all the time. I can keep in touch with family and friends, but I can also use it to keep in touch with God. How? Because the whole Bible is on my phone! It's an always available resource. But even without the Bible on a phone, we can still keep God's word, as the psalmist says, in our hearts. We can memorise Bible verses and keep them with us in that way. It means that the Bible is always with us in all circumstances, so that we have God's word to encourage and challenge us, or to share with others.

If everything else was taken away from us (think of Job) nobody can ever take God's word from our hearts. We might lose our keys, our phone or our Bible in a book form, but we still have God's word with us. I find that a great comfort.

Prayer: *Father God, thank you for giving us the Bible, and that you speak to us through it. Help us to learn the verses we need to live closely with you each day. Amen*

Thought for the day: Nothing can take God's word from my heart.

Pam Pointer (Wiltshire, England)

The ever-present source

Read Ephesians 3:14–19

I pray that, according to the riches of his glory, [the Father] may grant that you may be strengthened in your inner being with power through his Spirit.
Ephesians 3:16 (NRSV)

I looked on helplessly as a hummingbird that had flown into our office building tried desperately to get back out again. We eventually helped it to escape through a window, but during the ordeal it seemed to have used up nearly all of its strength with its fast-paced wing-flapping. The bird had grown progressively weaker because no food source was available to replenish its expended energy.

At times we are like that hummingbird. We find ourselves in sticky situations and flutter around frantically trying to find a way out. The frenetic activity saps our mental and emotional energy. Thankfully, we have a source of strength that is available to us, and we can tap into it to refuel our weary spirits so that we are enabled to go on. God is that source; in today's verse, Paul prayed for the people of the church in Ephesus that God's power would strengthen them.

In times of failing strength we, like Paul, can continually draw from God's ever-present and unlimited supply to keep our lives spiritually refreshed.

Prayer: *Dear God, help us to rely on your power that revives us when we become weary. Amen*

Thought for the day: God's supply of strength is always within reach.

Carol Dunn (Saint Andrew, Jamaica)

Forgive and forget?

Read Genesis 45:4–15

[The Lord says] I will forgive their iniquity, and remember their sin no more.
Jeremiah 31:34 (NRSV)

Today's Bible reading is about Joseph forgiving his brothers, but it is also clear that Joseph had not forgotten what his brothers had done. Although the command to 'forgive and forget' is not found specifically in the Bible, I still wish I could always forget. I can forgive small transgressions, and even forget most of them. Yet some hurtful memories continue to invade my heart and this makes me question whether or not I have truly forgiven the person involved.

But years ago, a TV programme about bees gave me a whole new perspective. When a beehive is invaded by an outsider, the bees protect the hive by stinging the invader to death. If the remains are too large to remove, they begin to cover them with layers of wax, so thick that the features become blurred and difficult to distinguish. And here is the wonderful part – the intruder becomes a lasting part of the hive!

This gave me an insight into forgiveness. I cannot completely remove hurtful invading memories. They are a part of my heart and who I am in Christ. But I can continually wrap them in layers of prayer and, with time, blur the hurtful details so that they no longer have power over me.

Prayer: *Compassionate God, thank you for the forgiveness we have in your Son. Help us to honour you today. Amen*

Thought for the day: Whatever pain enters my heart can help me grow in Christ.

Valerie L. Runyan (New Mexico, US)

God's quiet voice

Read 1 Kings 19:1–14

Now there was a great wind… but the Lord was not in the wind; and… an earthquake… and… a fire… and after the fire a sound of sheer silence.

1 Kings 19:11–12 (NRSV)

I am a social person, enjoying the company of others. Yet I find that my favourite hobbies occur in solitude: gardening, running in the woods or sitting quietly by the lake. At these times, I can be alone with my thoughts – pondering the day's devotional readings or formulating a subject for a sermon. Often during those times, inspiration strikes or I perceive God's direction.

I'm not alone in this perception. God first spoke to Samuel in the quiet of night. God made himself known to Elijah in the quiet aftermath of a great wind, an earthquake and a fire. The psalmist said, 'Be still before the Lord, and wait patiently for him' (Psalm 37:7, NIV). In our busy world, many distractions keep us from listening for God. It is important for each of us to find time each day to read God's word and then listen throughout our daily activities to hear his quiet voice, which leads us to understanding.

Prayer: *Dear God, help us to rid our thoughts of the useless distractions of this world. Fill our thoughts with your voice and our hearts with your love. Amen*

Thought for the day: I will find time today to listen for what God is saying to me.

Raymond Appel (Wisconsin, US)

Always connected

Read Ephesians 1:15–23

I have not stopped giving thanks for you, remembering you in my prayers.

Ephesians 1:16 (NIV)

When I found out that the car we had just bought had no CD player, I was disappointed. How would we listen to the music we loved on long drives? Then I discovered it had Bluetooth – a technology that uses radio waves to transmit sound wirelessly from paired devices near each other. When I paired the car's Bluetooth receiver with my tablet, I could play all the music I had on it. What amazed me was that the atmosphere around me was filled with waves that I could neither see, feel, taste nor smell. I could sense nothing. Yet the two Bluetooth devices would emit, detect, pick up and play these invisible waves back to me in words and melodies.

These invisible waves all around remind me of prayer. We have no idea who around us is praying for us or how many prayers are filling the atmosphere. But God does. Much as a Bluetooth receiver is tuned in to the device with which it is paired, God is tuned to our needs and always hears and receives our prayers.

Prayer: *Dear Father, help us to remember that we are always connected to you and that when we pray, you always hear us. Amen*

Thought for the day: God is as close as my prayers.

Violet Nesdoly (British Columbia, Canada)

Getting out of the boat

Read Matthew 14:22–33

[Jesus] said, 'Come.' So Peter got out of the boat, started walking on the water, and came towards Jesus.
Matthew 14:29 (NRSV)

One year, I stayed with a family who lived by a lake while I was doing a college summer school. When I told them I didn't know how to water ski, they were determined to teach me. This wasn't easy for me, not only because I did not have great balance but also because I was afraid of drowning. Frankly, I was scared even to get out of the boat. However, once I decided to climb out, I finally got up on the skis after a few tries (even though I could only keep my balance for a few seconds).

In today's reading, Jesus had gone off by himself to pray. The disciples were in a boat and had been pushed out to sea by the wind and the waves. Jesus began to walk towards them on the water, and at first the disciples thought he was a ghost. Peter said, 'Lord, if it is you, command me to come to you on the water' (Matthew 14:28).

Our youth leader used to tell us, 'You've got to get out of your comfort zone.' That's often what discipleship is like for us – doing things that are out of our comfort zones. We may be afraid and unsure, but still God says, 'Come.' As disciples, Jesus calls all of us out of the boat – out of the places we feel safest or most comfortable. We may falter, but Jesus is always there to catch us.

Prayer: *Dear Lord, grant us opportunities to follow you and the courage to step out of our comfort zones. Amen*

Thought for the day: Before I can follow Jesus, I have to get out of the boat.

Adam Benson (North Carolina, US)

Rejoice in every blessing

Read 1 Chronicles 16:34–36

Give thanks to the Lord, for he is good; his love endures forever.
1 Chronicles 16:34 (NIV)

When I saw the email, I braced myself. For nearly a year, I'd sent sample chapters to different publishers, praying that one of them would give me a contract for my novel. But so far I'd had only rejections – dozens of them – and this email proved to be another one.

A few days later, the publisher of an inspirational anthology accepted an essay I'd written, but I didn't enjoy the good news. When a friend congratulated me, my response was to complain that my novel had not been accepted. I later realised how ungrateful I was being. I was focusing on what I didn't have, rather than on God's blessings. Paul tells us, 'Always give thanks to God the Father for everything in the name of our Lord Jesus Christ' (Ephesians 5:20, CEB). God had answered my prayer – just not in the way I'd hoped. My essay would be read by the hundreds of people who bought the anthology. For that I am thankful.

Sometimes we can become so focused on one particular disappointment that we don't see the many blessings we receive every day. By being grateful for God's blessings even in the face of disappointing news, we are able to invite peace and joy into our lives and open our hearts to the many more blessings God has in store for us.

Prayer: *Dear God, give us grateful hearts that we may appreciate the work that you do in our lives. Amen*

Thought for the day: Being grateful helps me to recognise God's blessings.

Lisa Braxton (Massachusetts, US)

Towards the goal

Read Philippians 3:10–14

Forgetting what is behind and straining towards what is ahead, I press on towards the goal to win the prize for which God has called me heavenwards in Christ Jesus.
Philippians 3:13–14 (NIV)

Hokkaido, in Japan, is known for its racehorses. Once, when my family and I travelled there, a tour guide told us that some of the young horses were not obedient to their trainers, and that sometimes a foal is sent back to its home stud-farm and to its mother. The foal remembers her, but the mother doesn't remember the foal. In fact, when the foal approaches her, she often runs away. The trainer watches from a distance and at the moment the foal is left alone, the trainer calls to the foal in a strong, kind voice. At that point, the foal begins to see the trainer as a protector, a substitute for its mother. Then the foal changes and becomes obedient to the trainer.

When I heard this, I thought of the similarities between this horse–trainer relationship and our relationship with Jesus Christ. Before we meet him, we live the way we want to. But once we know that Christ has saved us, we feel a deep sense of peace and direction in our hearts. We stop looking at what is behind and instead press towards what lies ahead. As a good racehorse gallops on the track, we hope to finish the race, running towards the completion of our faith.

Prayer: *Father in heaven, thank you for sending your Son. Help us to grow in faith until we finish the race. Amen*

Thought for the day: 'I press on… because Christ Jesus has made me his own' (Philippians 3:12, NRSV).

Atsushi Nomiyama (Japan)

The best and worst of times

Read 2 Samuel 22:1–7

*[David sang,] 'In my distress I called to the Lord; I called out to my God.
From his temple he heard my voice; my cry came to his ears.'*
2 Samuel 22:7 (NIV)

When my husband was diagnosed with a brain tumour, we looked
death in the face. Yet, out of the ugliness of scalpels and scans, healthy
tissue destroyed with disease, muscle weakness, weight loss, nausea
and fatigue grew increased gratefulness for daily strength and the
meeting of our basic needs.

The Bible's declaration of God's never-failing presence moved from
our heads to our hearts, and we began living out our faith in new
and different ways. Employment lost became family time gained. We
learned to appreciate the present rather than constantly planning for
what could be. We recognised the futility of worry and the value of joy
in every circumstance. Whether good times or bad, we shared them
with one another and with our God who never leaves us alone. Fearful
that our walk as a couple might soon end, we clung to God's promise to
walk with us, whatever the future held.

Although struggles persist and the future remains unknown, through
trials we can become 'mature and complete' or even wise (see James
1:2–12). And no matter what, God is working through our trials to bring
out the good (see Romans 8:28).

Prayer: *Mighty God, remind us that pain and problems do not preclude
peace, and that hard times cannot conquer hope. Amen*

Thought for the day: Times of trial can give me new insight into God's
love for me.

Diana C. Derringer (Kentucky, US)

Freedom!

Read Exodus 6:1–7

It is for freedom that Christ has set us free. Stand firm, then, and do not let yourselves be burdened again by a yoke of slavery.
Galatians 5:1 (NIV)

As a black man living in the United States, I consider freedom one of my most precious blessings. My ancestors were slaves once, bought and sold like property, worked like cattle and sometimes beaten to the point of death. My ancestors could only dream of the freedom I was born with. It is never far from my thoughts that if I had been born 200 years ago, I couldn't do any of the things I am doing with my life today. I am a free man, and no matter how busy or stressed I get, I always take time to cherish and give thanks for this powerful truth.

Free. We use the word carelessly, often for food we didn't pay for or buy-one-get-one-free offers that give us even more stuff which we don't really need. Yet the power in that word should never be underestimated. I was born free. Maybe that's why, when the word of God tells me that all people everywhere were born into slavery to selfishness and sin and that Jesus died to set us free, I can barely choke back the tears. Each of us wore shackles around our necks, powerless against sin and death. And because Christ died for us, the chains are removed and we are let go – free to believe in, trust and follow Jesus.

Prayer: *Dear Jesus, thank you for giving your life to set us free. Help us to share this gift with all those who are still in bondage. Amen*

Thought for the day: Freedom from sin and death is a true treasure from God.

Gary Mitchell (North Carolina, US)

Answered prayer

Read 1 John 5:11–15

Call on me in the day of trouble; I will deliver you, and you shall glorify me.
Psalm 50:15 (NRSV)

A few years ago, one of my sons, Bongue, and I left home early one morning to attend a training seminar for ministers in Luanda. It was still dark. We had only walked a short way when we were approached by three thieves who demanded our wallets. When we resisted, they threatened us with a firearm and beat us. Then they took our wallets, belongings and money.

For several weeks, I felt hatred and fear, but I prayed constantly for God to touch the hearts of the people who had hurt us and, if possible, to see that my wallet was returned. Six months later, three people appeared at the church where my other son Abraham was the minister, and handed him my wallet, repenting of their evil acts and asking Abraham to pray for them and receive them into the church.

God had worked a miracle! He hears our prayers and answers them. We must never forget Jesus' promise: 'I am with you always, to the end of the age' (Matthew 28:20, NRSV).

Prayer: *Thank you, God, for your love and protection in difficult times. Teach us to pray without ceasing. We pray in the name of Jesus Christ, who taught us to pray: 'Our Father in heaven, hallowed be your name, your kingdom come, your will be done on earth as it is in heaven. Give us today our daily bread. And forgive us our debts, as we also have forgiven our debtors. And lead us not into temptation, but deliver us from the evil one.'* Amen*

Thought for the day: 'Love your enemies and pray for those who persecute you' (Matthew 5:44, NRSV).

Eunice Arão Kakueka (Luanda, Angola)

PRAYER FOCUS: SOMEONE WAITING FOR AN ANSWER TO PRAYER
*Matthew 6:9–13, NIV

Childlike faith

Read Psalm 121:1–8

The priests could not perform their service because of the cloud, for the glory of the Lord filled the temple of God.
2 Chronicles 5:14 (NIV)

When I was a child, I thought that God was actually in the streams of light that sometimes break through the clouds in the sky. It seemed to me that he was trying to reach down from heaven to earth to comfort and reassure us even on cloudy and overcast days. In the time since those naive childhood days, I've learned that those rays of light are just the sunbeams breaking through.

As I have matured in my faith, however, I've returned to some elements of my childlike wonder. I have come to believe that God is present in all things – even in the streams of light that sometimes break through the clouds. I see God reaching out to me in so many ways: through nature, in good and bad circumstances, my friends, through my church family and, most importantly, through scripture. I am especially thankful that God still pursues someone like me who thinks she already has everything all worked out.

Prayer: *Dear Father, open our eyes to see you everywhere we are and in everything we do. Give us a childlike faith that longs for your presence. We pray through Jesus, our Saviour. Amen*

Thought for the day: I can always learn something new about God.

Darlene S. Mackey (Tennessee, US)

PRAYER FOCUS: THOSE WHO CAN'T SENSE GOD'S PRESENCE

Keep praying

Read Matthew 21:18–22

[Jesus] left [the disciples] and went away once more and prayed the third time.
Matthew 26:44 (NIV)

I had invited my friend and his wife to attend church with me for some time, but they had never shown any interest in coming. For a long time they had been on my prayer list as I asked God to lead them to the church. Many times my friend and I had discussed religion, but church always seemed unimportant to him.

When he had heart surgery, friends took turns to support him and his wife. We showed them a concern that our words could not express. Not long after his surgery, I visited him and mentioned an event that was happening at church the next day. He told me that he and his wife had been thinking about going back to church, and the next day I was happy to see them there. For years now, they have attended regularly and have been faithful volunteers.

I remember that in Gethsemane, Jesus prayed multiple times. And the apostle Paul admonished us to pray without ceasing. When we persevere in prayer and never give up, but continue to ask in prayer with faith, God will answer.

Prayer: *Dear heavenly Father, help us to continue praying faithfully, trusting that you will respond. Amen*

Thought for the day: I will be persistent in my prayers.

James R. Hayes (Tennessee, US)

Giving grace

Read 2 Samuel 22:29–31

[God's] way is perfect: The Lord's word is flawless; he shields all who take refuge in him.
2 Samuel 22:31 (NIV)

I have always been very confident in my abilities. When I finished high school, I was sure I would get into university; however, I did not get good enough exam results. Because my plans were not working out, I wondered if God still cared about me. But the Lord wisely led me another way: I was able to study in another college where I could work and live closer to my family. That, in turn, gave me opportunities to show them the word of God.

As I prepared to graduate after a course of study that I truly enjoyed, I realised that I could never have completed my education alone. The opportunity of having the added years to deepen my relationship with my family and others allowed me to appreciate what is special in each one of them. Now, I thank God for not answering my prayer in the way that I had wanted. Not being able to fulfil my will at that time resulted in better circumstances. I have learned the power in using the gifts and talents God has given me to help others as much as I can.

Prayer: *Thank you, wise and loving God, for not acting according to our will but instead showing us your way. Help us to have open hearts to listen and obey. In the name of Jesus. Amen*

Thought for the day: Today as I make personal decisions, I will listen for the voice of the Lord.

Bruna Messias Rodrigues de Souza (Minas Gerais, Brazil)

Batteries included

Read Psalm 118:24–29

This is the day that the Lord has made; let us rejoice and be glad in it.
Psalm 118:24 (NRSV)

As a child, I celebrated birthdays with joy and excitement. I opened my
gifts with great zeal – ripping through wrapping paper, tearing open
boxes and turning gift bags upside down. I was particularly delighted
with gifts I could enjoy straight away, those labelled 'batteries included'.

The verse above describes another precious gift: the present day. It
too comes filled and ready to enjoy. The psalmist writes that the Lord
has made the day and encourages people to celebrate it with joy and
gladness. While the psalmist was recalling a specific day in Hebrew history, the call to celebrate the present day is for all people in all times.
The Lord has placed inside each day all that is needed for enjoyment
and spiritual growth. No batteries are required to appreciate this gift.

So often we miss the joy of today because we are preoccupied
with plans for tomorrow. How different life would be if we, with childlike zeal, turned the 'gift bag' of today upside down to get everything
out! While asking for tomorrow's needs, we can also pray for the Lord
to help us to be grateful for the present day and to look for all that is
placed inside it for us.

Prayer: *Dear Lord, help us to pause and appreciate the gift of today,
and to make the most of what it brings as we seek to serve you. Amen*

Thought for the day: I will show my gratitude to God for the gift of
each day.

Donyale Fraylon (Texas, US)

Work in process

Read Philippians 1:3–11

He who began a good work in you will carry it on to completion until the day of Christ Jesus.
Philippians 1:6 (NIV)

Before retiring a few years ago, I worked for a large food company. We sold many different types of products but used the same process to create them. We started with raw materials, and the completed product ready to be sold was known as 'finished product inventory'. The term applied to the steps in between – where raw materials were being processed but not yet finished – was 'work in process'. It was product that was partially made but not yet completed.

It occurs to me that those terms are a good analogy for our Christian walk. We all start out as 'raw materials'. When we accept Christ as our Saviour, we become a 'work in process'. We are born again and we begin the lifetime journey of becoming more like Christ. We look forward to the day when we will become a 'finished product', a citizen in heaven where Christ 'will transform our lowly bodies so that they will be like his glorious body' (Philippians 3:21, NIV).

Prayer: *Heavenly Father, thank you for the gift of your Son, Jesus Christ. Help us to live each day following the example of his life. In Jesus' name, we pray. Amen*

Thought for the day: Each day is an opportunity to become more like Christ.

John D. Bown (Minnesota, US)

Keep it simple

Read Isaiah 9:1–7

The people who walked in darkness have seen a great light.
Isaiah 9:2 (NRSV)

Recently, I was standing in a queue at the bank listening to both the counter assistant and a customer complaining to each other about the stress of the Christmas season. I then walked into the supermarket, where a dear friend also began to complain about the busyness of Christmas. 'There is so much to do: presents to choose and buy, food to prepare and so many functions to attend. Christmas is just one big headache,' she said. I replied, 'But I love Christmas and I especially love the four weeks of Advent!'

During the four weeks of Advent, we play Advent music in our home and in our car. We keep the food preparation and present-buying simple. We enjoy local community events. We make an effort to reach out to others and bless them, especially those who find this season difficult. During Advent and Christmas we find numerous ways to welcome the Christ child into our homes and into our lives.

Amid all the preparations and activities, we can enjoy the season of Advent and Christmas by keeping it simple as we prepare to welcome Jesus, the greatest gift of all.

Prayer: *Lord Jesus, prepare our hearts this Advent. Help us to open our eyes to the joy of your coming into the world and to focus on the true meaning of Christmas. Amen*

Thought for the day: This Advent, I will keep it simple by focusing on the Christ child.

Barb Sanders (South Australia, Australia)

Another way

Read Exodus 15:1–6

Moses stretched out his hand over the sea, and… the Lord drove the sea back with a strong east wind and turned it into dry land.
Exodus 14:21 (NIV)

One morning our automatic garage-door opener was broken. When I told five-year-old Ava to get into the car so I could take her to school, she reluctantly went to the car, but returned quickly after pressing the button and noticing that the door did not open. Sounding hopeless and with tears streaming down her face, she said, 'If we go into the garage we will be trapped. We won't be able to get out!' When I walked into the garage and manually opened the door, she settled down and took her seat. As Ava dried her tears, I assured her that I would never send her to a place where she could be trapped, lost or hurt.

This moment of reassuring Ava brought the Israelites to mind. What must they have felt as they stood at the edge of the Red Sea, just before God parted it? Like Ava in trying to open the garage door, I realise that I too sometimes need to hear words of reassurance – especially when my attempts to cope seem feeble and insufficient. I need to hear that God will truly never leave me or forsake me and that even when I am at the edge of my 'Red Sea', hotly pursued, God can make an unseen way clear.

Prayer: *Dear God, when we cannot see the way forward, help us to trust that you will make a way clear. Amen*

Thought for the day: God promises never to leave us or forsake us (see Deuteronomy 31:6, Hebrews 13:5).

Cassius Rhue (South Carolina, US)

PRAYER FOCUS: SOMEONE STRUGGLING TO TRUST GOD   103

Chemistry class

Read Psalm 19:1–6

God saw all that he had made, and it was very good.
Genesis 1:31 (NIV)

I grew up attending a Christian school and I had a religious instruction class every day. Often we were asked how we saw God in our lives. Every time I would give the same answer: I saw God in my family and in nature. I never really took the question seriously, so I didn't take the time to reflect on where I saw God in my life.

One day in my chemistry class we learned about the complex electron configurations of atoms. In my frustration at attempting to solve a difficult equation, I thought, 'Who made this so complicated?' Then I realised that the same One who created the atoms created every part of our world. God made this planet with water to drink, plants to eat and fresh air to breathe. And Earth is the perfect distance from the sun for humanity to survive.

I had already appreciated the God I could see in nature, but I had to look deeper to realise how amazing he is in creating all these complex elements that work together in perfect harmony.

Prayer: *Dear God, thank you for this beautiful world that you have created. Help us to find your love and compassion in every corner of it. Amen*

Thought for the day: The more places I look, the more I can see an amazing God.

Ali Southard (North Carolina, US

Our gifts

Read 1 Chronicles 29:14–18

We have given you only what comes from your hand.
1 Chronicles 29:14 (NIV)

I don't remember how old I was, but it was the first year I shopped for Christmas gifts on my own. My parents gave me some money and let me walk to some shops close to our house. I walked into a gift shop and laid my coins on the counter. The assistant helped me pick out a costume-jewellery brooch and a purple scarf for my mother. That Christmas, for the first time, I was as eager to see my mother open her gift as I was to open my own gifts.

Looking back, I am thankful for the assistant who spent so much time helping me. I have also had this thought: 'I could give my mother nothing that hadn't been given to me.' She certainly could have bought far nicer things for herself. Nevertheless, I think she was highly pleased to receive my gift.

In the same way, we can give nothing to God that didn't come from him in the first place. All our possessions, all our power, all our talents are gifts from God. Nevertheless, I believe that he is pleased by what we give.

Prayer: *O God, thank you for all the gifts you have given us. Thank you for allowing us to offer something in return. Amen*

Thought for the day: By giving to others, I show gratitude to God.

Drew Sappington (Florida, US)

Sweet peace

Read John 16:15–33

[Jesus said,] 'I have told you these things, so that in me you may have peace. In this world you will have trouble. But take heart! I have overcome the world.'
John 16:33 (NIV)

While my husband's Uncle Jim was in hospital awaiting open-heart surgery, he received the shocking news that his only son had been instantly killed in a logging accident. Jim was inconsolable. 'Why not me instead of him?' he cried out to God. When it seemed he had no more tears to shed, a gentle calm came over him. 'It was as if the Holy Spirit surrounded me,' Jim explained, 'and my troubled spirit finally rested. I still didn't understand why, but I did have the assurance that my boy was safe with my heavenly Father and I experienced a peace that only God could bring.'

Not long before his death, Jesus told his disciples that a time would come when their faith would be tested to the point of abandoning him. But he also assured them that they would find peace, be united by a strengthened faith and ultimately share in his victory.

That seems to be the journey often experienced by Christ's followers when trouble strikes – first shock and despair, but after a while the calming sense of the Holy Spirit's presence and the comforting awareness, 'We are not alone!' A welcome peace eventually comes – just as Jesus promised. But no matter what our circumstances, God is still with us, and we will share in his ultimate victory.

Prayer: *Gracious God, thank you for your steadfast love. Sustain us in difficult times. Amen*

Thought for the day: God never abandons me.

Gerri Nicholas (Alberta, Canada)

Rejoicing in a barren field

Read Habakkuk 3:17–19

Though the produce of the olive fails, and the fields yield no food… yet I will rejoice in the Lord.

Habakkuk 3:17–18 (NRSV)

Farmers work hard to ensure that their toil will be rewarded, that their families and communities will be well nourished. Yet no matter how diligent the labourer, sometimes crops will fail. All farmers, all prophets and all people face circumstances beyond their control.

The book of Habakkuk was written in the midst of a difficult season in Israel's history – the Assyrians attacking them and the Babylonian conquest looming. In the first two chapters of Habakkuk we find the prophet struggling in prayer with these difficult issues. At times he even questioned God. In the end, Habakkuk chose to worship the Lord and found joy in God's holy presence instead of in his circumstances.

I can relate to this. I have applied for jobs I didn't get, tried my best at relationships that did not work out and poured all my strength into ministry, only to see my dreams go unfulfilled for a time. I have learned that if our joy is found in results or in our present circumstances, then we will continually second-guess ourselves and face deep frustration. But if our strength and hope are in the Lord, then even in a barren season we will be able to follow Habakkuk's example and worship God with joy.

Prayer: *Dear Father, give us the perspective and the faith to praise you in the barren seasons of life. Amen*

Thought for the day: Even in stressful circumstances, I can find joy in God.

Phillip Catterton (Kansas, US)

We can pray

Read Romans 12:9–13

Do not be anxious about anything, but in every situation, by prayer and petition, with thanksgiving, present your requests to God.
Philippians 4:6 (NIV)

As Christians, we spend much time wrestling with difficult scripture, debating grey areas and trying to find God's direction in our lives. While all these efforts are important, sometimes we tend to miss the most obvious answer before us: prayer. How often do we look at our world, grieve internally for the chaos, assign blame and then forget to pray? We may feel completely helpless, not knowing what to do. Sometimes God calls us to take action, to drop everything and be on the front lines of solving the problems. At other times, all we can do is pray. Often, we can do both.

We all face important decisions in our personal lives, decisions that provoke uncertainty or anxiety. If only God gave us simple instructions to follow! But scripture does: 'Do not be anxious about anything, but in every situation, by prayer and petition, with thanksgiving, present your requests to God. And the peace of God... will guard your hearts and your minds in Christ Jesus.'

Life is uncertain. But even if everything else is stripped away from us, we can choose to pray.

Prayer: *Almighty God, may we never forget that prayer brings us close to you and that you are the source of our strength and peace. Amen*

Thought for the day: In the midst of turmoil, prayer brings me peace.

Katherine Brock (Georgia, US)

A piece of Christmas

Read Luke 2:8–20

When [the shepherds] saw [Jesus], they made known what had been told them about this child.
Luke 2:17 (NRSV)

Many years ago, before email and Skype, I worked at the local telegraph office in my home town. For several years I delivered telegrams on Christmas Eve to families whose husbands and children were away from home. After receiving a telegram, people often said, 'Wait, we can't let you go just like that, without a little piece of our Christmas!' And then they would give me an apple, an orange or some sweets.

At that time, Christmas was a personal family holiday. After a brief visit to church, we celebrated behind closed doors as a family. But there is nothing private about Christmas. The good news of the birth of Jesus is for people around us and throughout the world.

The presence of Jesus is our greatest hope. In Jesus there is hope that people of different nationalities and beliefs can understand and respect each other. In him we have hope that families who have experienced pain and tragedy will be able to be reconciled and draw closer to each other. In Jesus we have hope that we can leave behind all mistakes, regrets and sins and be reconciled with God. So we need not hesitate in bringing a piece of the good news of Christmas to everyone we meet today and throughout the New Year.

Prayer: *Loving God, thank you for the joy of Christmas. Help us to share that joy with others. Amen*

Thought for the day: How will I share a piece of the good news today?

Hans Vaxby (Helsinki, Finland)

Sharing what I have

Read Matthew 25:34–40

The King will reply, 'Truly I tell you, whatever you did for one of the least of these brothers and sisters of mine, you did for me.'
Matthew 25:40 (NIV)

As I left a restaurant one night, I saw a man silhouetted in the dim glow of a street light. He had scruffy hair, wore ill-fitting clothing and was carrying some plastic bags. Nervous, I tried to avoid eye contact as I walked by. But just as I passed him, the man pointed to the takeaway box I had brought with me from the restaurant and asked, 'Ma'am, are you going to eat that?' I paused and handed him the box, saying, 'Please take it.' I continued on to my car, surprised at what had happened. When I looked back, I saw the man already eating my dinner leftovers.

That night I made a silent promise that I would never again close my heart to someone I saw on the street, even if all I had to give was a kind word or leftovers from a meal. I cannot save everyone in the world from hunger, but God isn't asking me to do that. He does ask me to help those I can by sharing what I have. He doesn't want us to ignore another's suffering and walk by but to give with open hearts and open hands.

Prayer: *Heavenly Father, thank you for loving us all, despite our circumstances. Strengthen us to share your love and kindness with our hurting world. Amen*

Thought for the day: I can be God's hands and feet in the world.

Wilma R. Vernich (Tennessee, US)

God is good

Read Psalm 13:1–6

I will sing to the Lord because he has been good to me.
Psalm 13:6 (CEB)

On my 60th birthday, I sent my sister an email that said, 'I'm healthy, happy, married to a great man and I own a business caring for animals. Praise God, my dreams have come true!'

My birthday wasn't always a cause for celebration. On my 40th birthday, I was depressed, lived alone, working at two jobs and struggling with money worries. When I contemplated my future, it brought fears of relentless struggles with loneliness and hopelessness. I did not celebrate on my 40th birthday. I felt only deep sadness.

My fears and sadness were transformed into hopefulness several months later when I began attending church. I went to seek God's solace and I received his mercy and grace. I made Christian friends. I met my husband while serving on a mission-ministry team. And I launched a successful pet-care business.

God can deliver us from the fears that smother our hope, but his blessings require our participation. Psalm 34:8 invites us to 'Taste and see that the Lord is good' (NIV). Seeking God can transform our lives.

Prayer: *God of goodness and grace, thank you for delivering us from our fears. Amen*

Thought for the day: God can transform my sadness into hope.

Debra Pierce (Massachusetts, US)

The glory of the lowly

Read Exodus 39:32–43

All the work of the tabernacle of the tent of meeting was finished; the Israelites had done everything just as the Lord had commanded Moses.
Exodus 39:32 (NRSV)

When we had our first baby, I became a stay-at-home mum. It was the job I had always longed for. So why was I constantly plagued by feelings of low self-esteem and futility? It was partly because I spent too much time comparing myself to others. But it was also because I was failing to measure my worth by God's standards.

Today's reading about constructing the tabernacle in the wilderness tells us something about worth. When the Israelites had completed all the components, they presented their work to Moses for inspection. He didn't ask to see only the ark of the covenant and the pure gold lampstands; he asked to see every last piece of this important structure. Aaron's priestly garments had to be perfect, but so did the tent pegs. In God's eyes, each item was important and each was infused with value and significance.

Sometimes I may not feel like anything more than a peg, holding down the flapping tent of my home, my job or my life. But in God's eyes it is not important whether we are made of bronze or gold. Instead, we give glory to God by carrying out the worthy and vital purpose for which he designed us.

Prayer: *Dear Lord, help us to view our tasks through your eyes and, in doing so, glorify you with our attitudes and actions. Amen*

Thought for the day: When I measure my worth by God's standards, I am always enough.

Esther MacDonald (Quebec, Canada)

Worth it

Read Matthew 4:18–22
Immediately they left the boat and their father and followed him.
Matthew 4:22 (NIV)

When I was younger, I felt called to follow God instead of my friends. Trying to get me to go out with them instead of attending Bible study, my friends would say things like, 'You can go next week' or 'Do you actually believe in that stuff?' I would tell them, 'I know that I would not have many of the good things in my life if it were not for God and the relationship I have built with him through Bible study.' Even though my friends criticised me and left me out of things because of my decision, I would go every week to Bible study. I knew I was doing the right thing. I ended up knowing much more about God than my friends did, and when we were teenagers my friends started asking me questions about my faith.

Not everyone chooses to follow God, perhaps because it seems that doing so means having to give up so much. But what we give up for our faith is far less fulfilling than what we gain by living faithfully. Choosing to follow Christ may seem difficult in the beginning, but it is worth it in the end.

Prayer: *Dear Lord, guide us to do what is right and to help others. As Jesus taught us, we pray, 'Father, hallowed be your name, your kingdom come. Give us each day our daily bread. Forgive us our sins, for we also forgive everyone who sins against us. And lead us not into temptation.'* Amen*

Thought for the day: God will lead me to what is important.

Collin Clarke (North Carolina, US)

Our refuge and strength

Read Psalm 46:1–11

God is our refuge and strength, an ever-present help in trouble.
Psalm 46:1 (NIV)

Ice skimmed the surface of the pond. Summer's leaves had fallen from the willow branches and now, barely mirrored in the frozen water, they hung stark and drab. A cluster of ducks huddled together and a small army of geese patrolled the banks, looking for food.

Holding the hand of a small child, a man crouched beside the water throwing crumbs to the geese. Hissing with aggression, necks out-stretched, the geese broke ranks and scrambled to get to the food first. Protectively, the father drew the child close, away from the geese, so that he would be safe. The tenderness of the father towards his child reminded me of God's love for us, his children. 1 John 3:1 says: 'See what great love the Father has lavished on us, that we should be called children of God! And that is what we are!' (NIV).

Sometimes the world can seem a cold and unsympathetic place. But do we feel unloved, abandoned? Never! In Deuteronomy 32:10 we read: '[God] shielded [his people]… as the apple of his eye.' God is our refuge and our strength; he supports us through all circumstances, and his love never wavers.

Prayer: *Dear Lord, thank you for your loving care. Thank you for being our refuge and strength. Amen*

Thought for the day: God's great love for us will never change.

Pauline Pullan (North Yorkshire, England)

Trust

Read Jeremiah 29:10–14

'I know the plans I have for you,' declares the Lord, 'plans to prosper you and not to harm you, plans to give you hope and a future.'
Jeremiah 29:11 (NIV)

Though I'm only 16 years old, I haven't missed the reality that today's world is full of terror and violence. No matter what goes on in my life, it seems as if those factors are some of the only constants. I cannot recall the last time I woke up and didn't see a headline about a shooting or another act of terror. At times I find it easy to be consumed by the darkness and it is hard to see the light of God and hold onto hope for the future.

At school, I am beginning to be asked what I want to do in the future. I hesitate before answering because, honestly, I don't know what I want to do. Today's scripture reading reminds me that the Lord has a plan for everyone. God created each of us to fulfil a purpose. I often find myself wondering, 'What is my purpose? How does God want me to change the world?' Even though I don't yet know the path that God wants me to take, I find a certain joy in knowing that he has a plan for me.

God has a purpose for each of us in this world – for peace not war, for love not hatred. Each of us can find peace in learning to open our hearts to trust God's will.

Prayer: *Dear Lord, help us to recognise the gifts you have given us and to trust that you will use them to make the world a more loving place. Amen*

Thought for the day: I find peace when I trust in God's purpose for my life.

Noah Saffer (North Carolina, US)

He will come!

Read Isaiah 40:1–5

A voice cries out: 'In the wilderness prepare the way of the Lord.'
Isaiah 40:3 (NRSV)

The tiny church in which I grew up didn't have a regular minister, so one had to come from another town. The travel was often precarious, and sometimes our visiting minister was unable to make the trip. Every month we waited, hoping that he would be able to come and preside over our Communion service, but we sometimes would go three months without his presence. I still remember the dedication of the brothers and sisters who prepared the table with the elements for Communion, not knowing if we would be able to celebrate the sacrament, since in our tradition a minister must serve it.

Just as my church prepared itself for that momentous celebration of the Christian faith, Advent reminds us of our waiting for the Son of God. Advent is a time to prepare the way of the Lord. The crooked roads shall become straight and the rough ways smooth. A child will be born! Something eternally significant will come to all the people and all will know the way to an abundant life.

Prayer: *Gracious God, we open ourselves once again to welcome your blessed Son as our Saviour. In his name we pray. Amen*

Thought for the day: What can I do today to prepare the way for the Lord?

Edson Alves (Minas Gerais, Brazil)

In joy and in sorrow

Read Matthew 6:25–34

Do not worry, saying, 'What will we eat?' or 'What will we drink?' or 'What will we wear?' For... your heavenly Father knows that you need all these things.
Matthew 6:31–32 (NRSV)

In June 2016, my beloved husband of 37 years passed away. He was diagnosed with pancreatic cancer, given perhaps six months to live, and sent home with nursing care on a Friday. On the following Tuesday he died, and my life came crashing down. I felt buffeted by shock, grief, pain, tears and loneliness. Moreover, I was overwhelmed by the responsibilities of caring for the house, the car and all the other aspects of the life that we had shared. I knew God was with me but grief consumed me.

In January, a massive storm blew into our town, rattling windows, breaking tree branches and causing feelings of restlessness. I sat and watched the swirling chaos and noticed that my bird feeder was being tossed by the wind. I thought, 'Lord, that is how I feel. I am hanging on and being rocked by all this wind of chaos in my life.'

Suddenly, I noticed two little sparrows feeding at the bottom of the feeder. In spite of all the swaying, they were calm. And then I felt God say to me, 'Just as I am with these birds who are protected from the raging wind, so I have been with you, protecting you in this storm of grief. I have fed you with love, comfort, peace, the support of family and friends, and the guidance and the presence of the Holy Spirit. I will never leave you or forsake you.' I knew then that, whether in joy or in sorrow, we are not alone. God is with us.

Prayer: *Gracious and merciful God, thank you for being with us in our joy and in our sorrow. Amen*

Thought for the day: Even in my deepest grief, God is present.

Nina Semingson (Washington, US)

Trust in God

Read 1 Samuel 17:32–50

David said to the Philistine, 'You come against me with sword and spear and javelin, but I come against you in the name of the Lord Almighty, the God of the armies of Israel, whom you have defied.'
1 Samuel 17:45 (NIV)

In today's reading, David, a young shepherd, faced the challenge of fighting Goliath. No one believed that David could defeat Goliath, but David told King Saul that God had helped him defend his flock of sheep from lions and bears and would rescue him from Goliath too. David declined to wear the battle armour that King Saul gave him and went to meet Goliath with only a staff, a slingshot, five stones and trust in God. David defeated Goliath, not because of strength or skill but because he faced his enemy in the name of the Lord.

Sometimes we may feel desperate in difficult situations because we can find no solutions. We may feel too small to face the great problems of life. At times like these, whether we are young in faith or leaders in the church, we can put our trust in God.

David knew that the king's armour would not give him victory. It is not by strength, intelligence, wealth or influence that we will succeed. Victory lies only in the Lord who is with us at all times.

Prayer: *Dear God, thank you for your protection. Help us to trust in you so that we can overcome the obstacles of our lives. We pray in Jesus' name. Amen*

Thought for the day: With God I can conquer anything.

Hochai Adriano (Luanda, Angola)

Above the clamour

Read Luke 5:12–16

Jesus often withdrew to lonely places and prayed.
Luke 5:16 (NIV)

Exhausted and close to tears, I looked down at a table full of the gold-painted flower pots I was making into angels as gifts for teachers and staff members at my daughters' school. I had a hundred angels before me and no peace in my heart, I thought. Good intentions led me to agree to help with this project, but after adding it to my usual routine and Christmas activities, I was coming close to my breaking point. But I thought, 'If I don't do it, who will?' I was confusing busyness with holiness, wants with needs and personal pride with ministry.

Whenever I find myself overwhelmed by busyness, I remember that Jesus took time away from the crowds to be alone with God. Afterwards, Jesus would return to his disciples refreshed, strengthened and refocused – able to hear God's voice above the clamour of other demands and to be effective in ministry.

If Jesus needed time alone with God, how much more do we? May we follow Jesus' example by making time to be alone with God, so we too may be refreshed, strengthened and refocused to participate in his ministry.

Prayer: *Dear God, we are grateful that you want to spend time with us. May we be faithful in putting you first in the midst of our busy lives. Amen*

Thought for the day: Today I will take time away from busyness to be alone with God.

Kim Rumsey (Virginia, US)

Obstacle or opportunity?

Read James 1:1–5

Yes, my soul, find rest in God; my hope comes from him.
Psalm 62:5 (NIV)

My hard work and long days of studying had finally paid off when
started the most challenging programme in the United States army
Then I began to struggle with work that was too fast-paced and com
pletely different from the way I had learned in the past. Believing tha
my self-worth was based on my performance, I tried very hard in ar
extremely stressful environment.

At first, I didn't understand why God would help me get to that poin
only to let me fail. Then I read a book about God's seasons and how
not every season revolves around increase. Some are about prepara
tion and some about ploughing. All serve an important purpose, anc
if we don't keep our eyes fixed on God's love for us, we run the risk o
missing that purpose. I was reminded that my self-worth has nothing
to do with my performance and everything to do with the approval tha
God has already given me. I am loved and valuable, regardless of the
season I'm in.

As a result, I started to encourage others and share the love of Goc
with those around me for the rest of my time there. God opened door
for me that I never imagined, and now I am happy to be on the path the
Lord is setting for me.

Prayer: *Dear Lord, give us the discernment to be thankful for ever*
season, and give us the strength to bring you glory through it all. Amer

Thought for the day: Where I see big obstacles, God sees big oppor
tunities.

David Westbrook (Connecticut, US

Standing firm

Read 1 Peter 4:12–19
Those who suffer according to God's will should commit themselves to their faithful Creator and continue to do good.
1 Peter 4:19 (NIV)

With knocking knees and a shaky voice, I spoke at a parenting conference. It was a huge step of faith for me to stand before a large crowd and share what God had taught me. But one man in the audience got upset. He wrote notes and made calls to remove me from continuing to speak at the conference, simply because I was a woman. He was successful and I was crushed. I didn't speak in front of another audience for months. My self-pity kept me silent and kept me from filling the role that God had designed for me.

It's strange how self-pity can become a comfortable habit. It can keep us from learning, growing and continuing to do good. Thankfully, God uses both our defeats and victories (see Romans 8:28).

Little by little, God helped me to regain my confidence and start speaking again. I learned that allowing self-pity to dictate my actions isn't a faithful response to challenges. When we are challenged for our faith – and we will be – it's best to keep on serving, trusting that God will bless us. God promises, 'Those who stand firm during testing are blessed. They are tried and true. They will receive the life God has promised to those who love him as their reward' (James 1:12, CEB).

Prayer: *Dear God, help us to trust you with every victory and every defeat. Thank you for using both for your purpose and glory. Amen*

Thought for the day: Though I may be suffering, I am a blessed child of God.

May Patterson (Alabama, US)

Listening between the lines

Read Psalm 125:1–4

Do not neglect to show hospitality to strangers, for by doing that some have entertained angels without knowing it.
Hebrews 13:2 (NRSV)

One thing that I discovered early in my ministry was to 'learn to listen between the lines' – to pay attention to more than just what is said.

This challenge was evident to me one day when I visited a woman in hospital. I asked her how she was feeling, and she answered, 'I am fine, thank you.' But as I looked at her I could see that she had tears in her eyes. So I asked her, 'Are you sure you really feel fine?' She then opened up to me and told me that she was worried and scared of what the future held. As we talked and prayed, I assured her that God would be with her, whatever the future might be.

A few days later when I returned to the hospital, that woman had a smile on her face. She thanked me for visiting and said that she now felt the peace of God within her. I was grateful that 'listening between the lines' had allowed me to know and to respond to her deeper feelings.

Prayer: *Dear Lord, keep us ever alert to help those on life's journey who are worried and afraid. We pray in the name of Jesus, whose love can cast out all fear. Amen*

Thought for the day: Whatever the future holds, God will be with me.

Jim MacLean (Queensland, Australia)

Looking to God

Read Deuteronomy 4:27–31

In your distress, when all these things have happened to you in time to come, you will return to the Lord your God and heed him.
Deuteronomy 4:30 (NRSV)

One year, I offered to help my youth leader by directing the Christmas carol service readers for the Christmas Eve service. Between the ages of ten and twelve, the children felt nervous about reading in front of the congregation. Beforehand the two girls and two boys asked me many questions, such as, 'How will I know when to move from my seat?' 'Do I go up to read as the carol is being sung or afterwards?' Finally, I understood that no matter how many times I explained what to do, they were going to worry. I told the four brave readers, 'If you're unsure of when to start reading, make eye contact with me, and I'll help you, so that you know what to do.' Since they did not know me, I doubted that they would trust me to guide them if they were unsure. Nevertheless, I offered my help, reassuring them that they were not alone. Sure enough, during the service each one looked my way.

To me, this is similar to our relationship with God. In times of trouble, we may forget that he is present to help us and give us courage. We can trust him for guidance in any situation. God's constant and wise presence will never fade.

Prayer: *Wonderful and ever-present God, help us to look to you for guidance, trusting in your love. Amen*

Thought for the day: I won't let fear stop me from looking to God.

Kelly Gaylord (North Carolina, US)

God is with me

Read Luke 1:26–35
'The virgin will conceive and give birth to a son, and they will call him Immanuel' (which means 'God with us').
Matthew 1:23 (NIV)

My Christmas preparations had come to a grinding halt. Chemotherapy had interrupted my annual sprint through my usual pre-Christmas activities. Instead of sending family and friends my usual Christmas letter, brimming with cheerful stories about children and pets, I announced that I had been diagnosed with cancer.

That year, I decorated sparsely. A simple hand-painted nativity set graced my lounge. Cancer surgery had prevented me from travelling during the Thanksgiving holiday, so I looked forward to visiting family for Christmas once I had finished the next round of chemotherapy.

As I sat in my childhood church on Christmas Eve, flames from the candles danced to the joyous music of Christmas carols being sung. The light filled the church. I realised that a light had shone in the darkness for me just as it had for the shepherds on the first Christmas night.

Despite my grappling with the unfamiliar world of cancer and chemotherapy, one thing hadn't changed: God sent us Jesus – Immanuel – as a baby born in a manger. Because Immanuel means 'God with us', I knew then that God was still with me.

Prayer: *Thank you, heavenly Father, that the truth of the Christmas message never changes. Amen*

Thought for the day: God is with me during the Christmas season and always.

Joanie Shawhan (Wisconsin, US)

Christmas perfection

Read Luke 2:1–7

[Mary] gave birth to her firstborn, a son. She wrapped him in cloths and placed him in a manger, because there was no guest room available for them.
Luke 2:7 (NIV)

Every year I dread the task of putting up the Christmas tree. The decade-old artificial tree is crooked – bushy on one side, bare on the other. The tinsel doesn't quite reach round the entire tree. One strand of the lights doesn't work. The star on top is slightly bent. It's a reminder of how imperfect, once again, the Christmas decorations will be.

Yet every year as I look at the tree, I think of how imperfect that first Christmas was – the imperfect circumstances of Mary's pregnancy before marriage, the imperfect location of Jesus' birth in a stable, and the imperfect bed Mary laid him in after his birth: a manger. Even the timing of his birth, during the Roman census, was imperfect. But in much the same way that my children's delight at having decorated this Christmas tree is perfect, God's plan for Jesus' arrival was perfect.

The gift of Jesus Christ to an imperfect people was God's plan. Even when we fall short time and time again, we can look to our heavenly Father and remember the perfect love he poured down for each of us through Jesus Christ.

Prayer: *Dear Lord, remind us that the imperfect circumstances that Mary went through resulted in a gift of perfect love for the world. Thank you for the gift of Jesus. Amen*

Thought for the day: Though I am imperfect, God's love for me isn't.

Gabrielle Meisel (Michigan, US)

PRAYER FOCUS: TO ACCEPT IMPERFECTION IN MYSELF AND OTHERS

The goldfish bowl

Read Matthew 7:1–5

Jesus looked at [the disciples] and said, 'For mortals it is impossible, but not for God; for God all things are possible.'
Mark 10:27 (NRSV)

When I was young, I wondered why so many people would want such small, unexciting creatures as goldfish for pets. Then on a school trip to a botanical garden, I saw a pond full of fish, and a brilliantly coloured one stood out to me. I was surprised to learn it was a goldfish. 'Aren't goldfish small?' I asked. 'Not at all,' our guide replied. 'Some goldfish will grow even larger than these. It depends on the size of their environment.'

Years later, I finally understand the broader lesson: our perception of the world can limit our understanding of the limitless possibilities Christ offers. How often have I been like a goldfish in a bowl, unable to see my potential for growth? Worse still, how often have I confined others to small bowls by writing them off as insignificant or unexciting?

My faith in Christ's power teaches me that I could achieve so much more if I could forget my perceived limitations and swim beyond the boundaries I have placed on myself. With a wider perspective, I could see others' potential to grow and could move them from small bowls to an ocean of possibilities. Just imagine a world full of people who believe that anything is possible through Christ and who reach out and claim it! Together we could do astonishing things.

Prayer: *God of endless possibilities, broaden our view of your world to see the uniqueness of all you have created. Amen*

Thought for the day: With Christ, my possibilities are limitless.

Nelson Nwosu Chidera Omoregbe (Anambra, Nigeria)

A mother's love

Read Psalm 20:1–9

[Jesus said,] 'How often have I desired to gather your children together as a hen gathers her brood under her wings, and you were not willing!'
Matthew 23:37 (NRSV)

Our family has a small flock of chickens. One spring, we watched our mother hen hatch six eggs. When the chicks were small, she was always busy trying to keep her brood together. One morning, we heard the hen making loud, strange noises, and we could tell that something wasn't right.

As our family rushed to the garden, we saw the mother hen standing in front of a small bush with her feathers fluffed up and her wings spread out as a hawk circled overhead. Her chicks were nowhere to be seen. Our boys started yelling and waving their arms to scare away the hawk, and my wife and I began to look for the chicks. At first we couldn't find them. Then they slowly began to emerge from under the bush where the mother hen had safely hidden them. In the face of danger, the hen had rushed out to face the hawk, putting the welfare of her family first.

In today's verse, Jesus compares himself to a protective mother hen. When I read these words, I often recall that day in our garden. Mothers all over the world display this kind of love, and Jesus demonstrated this sacrificial love when he died for the whole world on the cross. Because of Jesus, we know that God will sacrifice everything to love and protect us.

Prayer: *Loving God, help us to love others the way you love us. Amen*

Thought for the day: God will always love and protect me.

Geoffrey L. Snook (Kansas, US)

Heavenly Father

Read Ephesians 3:14–21

My God will meet all your needs according to the riches of his glory in Christ Jesus.
Philippians 4:19 (NIV)

I am Indian, but my grandson, Aryan, was born in Texas and later moved to Kansas. One day when he came back from Sunday school, he innocently said to his father, 'Dad, you are not my real father. God is my father, and he will take care of my needs.' He must have learned it from his Sunday school lesson.

When I heard him say this, my mind went back to the time when I confidently stated the same to my father. At the age of 17, I surrendered my life to Jesus and accepted his call to serve him full-time. All my siblings were well settled, but my father was a bit worried about my future. I remember telling my father that day with faith and confidence, 'Dad, my heavenly Father is the ruler of this universe. He will supply all my needs according to his riches. It's his promise to me.'

Now I am 67 years old; my vision is getting dim and my walk has slowed down. But with faith and hope, I stand even stronger than I was that day all those years ago. Yes, God is faithful to keep promises and will supply all our needs 'according to the riches of his glory in Christ Jesus'.

Prayer: *Thank you, heavenly Father, for being faithful to us and supplying all our needs. Amen*

Thought for the day: 'The Lord is my shepherd; I shall not want' (Psalm 23:1, KJV).

Sarala veni Prabhakar (Andhra Pradesh, South India)

Forgiving family

Read Colossians 3:12–17

Don't judge, and you won't be judged. Don't condemn, and you won't be condemned. Forgive, and you will be forgiven.
Luke 6:37 (CEB)

My family is high on my list of blessings. So these past few years have been painful for me both emotionally and spiritually. My family members and I have found ourselves in court, resorting to the legal system to resolve our differences. After many hours of praying fervently and trying to encourage resolution, I handed the situation over to God – realising that I could rely only on divine guidance.

Through this painful process, God showed me that I had to forgive myself for missing both the signs of serious conflict and the opportunities that might have helped resolve the issue. God also showed me that I needed to forgive my family members. When I read today's quoted verse, I saw clearly that Jesus gave these three commands together for a purpose. I had prided myself on forgiving, but was I also judging and condemning? Was I thinking of these family members as undeserving of God's mercy? Was I truly forgiving them?

As I reflected on those questions I remembered today's scripture reading, which encourages us to forgive as Christ forgave us and to do all in the name of Jesus. I knew that I had fallen short. Once we leave the judging and condemning to God, we can truly forgive.

Prayer: *Thank you, Lord, for the peace and relief we feel when we obey your instruction to forgive each other – and ourselves. Amen*

Thought for the day: Who is God calling me to forgive today?

Jacinta Fontanelle (Delaware, US)

God's glory

Read Psalm 16:1–11

You show me the path of life. In your presence there is fullness of joy; in your right hand are pleasures forevermore.
Psalm 16:11 (NRSV)

I have always found astronomy fascinating. I love to look up at the sky and see planets, stars and galaxies. I have even been able to show my daughters a few constellations. But I live in New Jersey and, no matter where I go, I cannot get away from all the lights.

Once when I was camping in the Rocky Mountains, the first night I looked up and said, 'Wow! What is that in the sky?' My friend told me that it was the stars of the Milky Way. I was awestruck. It was as if someone had hurled a bucket of glitter into the night sky! I had never seen such a sight before.

This experience made me think about my relationship with God. When I'm surrounded by the world's clutter and noise, giving God a quick glance, I see only a small part of who God is. Yet, when I get away from all the competing distractions and open my Bible in quiet contemplation, I see God's glory in all its magnificence. I feel his presence and peace, and once again I am awestruck. Whenever I spend time praying, fasting and digging deeply into the Bible, I am powerfully aware that I am in the presence of God.

Prayer: *Creator God, help us to seek your presence each and every day. Thank you for the many ways you reveal your glory to us. Amen*

Thought for the day: Today I will look for the wonder of God in creation.

Bob LaForge (New Jersey, US)

Celebrating God

Read Acts 2:41–47

Day by day, as they spent much time together in the temple, they broke bread at home and ate their food with glad and generous hearts.
Acts 2:46 (NRSV)

In our culture, we celebrate the end of the year with a New Year's Eve party with our friends. We always have an array of food and enjoy music, dancing and friendly conversation.

About three years ago, I joined a Christian church. We celebrate our year-end gatherings differently now. A small group from our church meets at my home. We continue to enjoy our delicious food but also make time for worship and singing praises to God. The best part is listening to our different stories of God's protection – the marvellous things he has accomplished in our lives throughout the year – and then giving thanks to him for it all. We are inspired by the Holy Spirit as we speak of what our faith means to us and of our abiding hope for the coming year. To be sure, we continue to learn and grow in our understanding of God. But we look to the future with faith and full assurance, determined to bear witness so that others will know and experience God's love and protection.

Prayer: *God of hope, we ask for your loving guidance and blessing wherever people gather to learn, worship and pray. Amen*

Thought for the day: Today I will tell others of my abiding hope in God.

Annabella Lemos Cernaz (Valle del Cuaca, Colombia)

Small group questions

Wednesday 5 September

1 When has someone shown you an act of uncommon kindness? What did the person do for you? What is most memorable from this experience?

2 Have you ever failed to do something for someone and then regretted it? How did you respond the next time you had the opportunity to show kindness to someone?

3 Who has been a role model for you when it comes to helping others in need? What would you say is the most important lesson this person has taught you?

4 Is there ever a time when it is okay not to help someone in need? If so, when?

5 Name three ways you will show 'uncommon kindness' to someone in the coming week.

Wednesday 12 September

1 How often do you ask for God's guidance in a situation? Do you think some situations or concerns are too small to take to him? If so, give an example. If not, why not?

2 When has God answered one of your prayers in a way that was contrary to your expectations? How did you respond to him? Did this experience change the way you pray? Did it affect your relationship with God?

3 When has God answered one of your prayers in the way that you hoped? Were you surprised that he answered your prayer this way? Why or why not?

4 How well do you deal with change and the unexpected? When have you experienced a change or something unexpected that challenged you in a significant way? How did God help you through this ordeal? What were your prayers like during this time?

5 Why do you think change can sometimes be so difficult? Do you think change is necessary and a fact of life or can it be avoided? What advice would you give to someone who does not cope well with change? What is your prayer today for someone struggling with change?

Wednesday 19 September

1 The writer of today's meditation says, 'I am reminded that being recognised, called by name and appreciated are blessings that I receive from God and from others.' When have you been reminded of this as well?

2 Is it easy or difficult for you to make new friends? Would you say the phrase 'quality, not quantity' is true when it comes to the number of friends we have? Explain.

3 Recall some friendships from the Bible. Which characteristics of these friendships would you like to have in your own friendships?

4 When has getting to know someone forced you out of your comfort zone? What specifically challenged you in the situation? What opportunities did it provide, and what did you learn from it?

5 Name some people in your community who are overlooked. What will you do to make them feel recognised and welcome?

Wednesday 26 September

1 Which household job or task is your least favourite? What do you dislike about it? How could you turn the time you spend doing this chore into a time of prayer?

2 Can you think of a time when you have had adjust your spiritual attitude? What was going on in your life? Looking back on the experience, how has it shaped your relationship with God?

3 The scripture quote of today's meditation is 1 Thessalonians 5:16–18. What do you think it means to 'pray without ceasing'?

4 Name some of the ways that God has blessed you. For which of these blessings are you particularly thankful?

5   Who is on your prayer list today? What is your prayer for them? For what would you like prayer?

Wednesday 3 October

1   Do you have a daily spiritual practice? If so, what is it? If not, what keeps you from having one? Do you think a daily spiritual practice is important?

2   Do you enjoy physical exercise? Do you see any relationship between physical health and spiritual health? Which of the two is more important?

3   What are the 'spiritual strengths' of your faith community? Why do you think God gives each of us different spiritual strengths?

4   Looking back on your life, what significant spiritual changes do you see in yourself? Were you aware of the changes at the time or do you see them only now that you are looking back?

5   What do you think the writer of today's meditation means when he says he 'found a greater awareness of God's presence'? How do you recognise God's presence in your life? How might you become more aware of his presence?

Wednesday 10 October

1   When has someone prayed for you during a difficult time? How do you think it affected the outcome of your situation?

2   Under what circumstances and in what situations do you offer to pray for others? Is this something that comes naturally to you or is it awkward? What if you offered to pray for someone and the person said no? How would you respond?

3   Is there ever a time when offering to pray for someone is inappropriate or unhelpful? If so, when?

4   Do you think it is possible to change God's mind through prayer? Explain. Support your answer with scripture.

5 Have you ever been surprised by the way God answered one of your prayers? Why did it surprise you? What did this teach you about prayer?

Wednesday 17 October

1 Which characters in scripture used their gifts in unique and amazing ways? Which of these is your favourite?

2 What spiritual gifts has God given you? Which of your gifts have others recognised and appreciated? How could you use your gifts to serve others better?

3 Who do you know who uses God's gifts fully? What spiritual gifts do you most admire in others? What gift do you wish you had that you do not? Why?

4 What are God's expectations of the ways in which we use our gifts? Are there any restrictions on how we can or should use the abilities God has given us?

5 Have you ever encountered someone who claims to have no special gifts or abilities? What words of wisdom and advice would you give to this person?

Wednesday 24 October

1 The writer of today's meditation says, 'Often, grief, setbacks or radically changed circumstances leave us uncertain and confused.' Think back on a time when this was true for you. What helped you get through the situation?

2 Have you ever had a problem that seemed as though it had no solution? What did you do? In what ways did your faith help you cope with the problem? What words of encouragement would you give to someone going through something similar?

3 When in your life has God brought something good out of a bad situation? What did this teach you about him and the troubles we face in life?

4 Do you think God is in control of everything that happens in the world? If so, why does he allow bad things to happen to us and to those we love? Support your answer with scripture.

5 Name two specific actions that you will commit to in the coming week to help someone going through a difficult time.

Wednesday 31 October

1 In the story of Mary and Martha, with which character do you identify most? Why? What is the most important lesson we can learn from the story?

2 How much time do you spend with God each day? In what ways does spending time with God equip us to serve him and others better?

3 Why do you think people often have negative things to say about Martha? Are those criticisms fair? Why or why not?

4 Describe a time when you have been 'distracted by many things' and overlooked what is most important. What did you learn about yourself from this experience? What will you do differently the next time you are in a similar situation?

5 Under what circumstances or in what settings do you find it easiest to focus on God? What disciplines or practices help you focus your attention on him? How does your church congregation support focused attention on God? How could it better support it?

Wednesday 7 November

1 When have you felt insignificant? What helped you regain your sense of significance? Who in your life do you think might feel insignificant? How will you help them feel more significant?

2 Is it okay for us to find our meaning and purpose in a job, money, where we live or who we know? Why or why not? What would you say to a person who looks for significance in these things?

3 The writer of today's meditation says, 'I realised that God can use each of us wherever we are.' Talk about a time when this has been

true for you. What did you learn about yourself that you did not know before?

4 When have you helped someone in an unexpected place and way? Do you think it was just a coincidence that you happened to be in the right place at the right time or did God have something to do with it? Explain.

5 Name some stories in scripture in which God used people where they were to fulfil a mission or purpose. Which of these stories do you find particularly meaningful and powerful?

Wednesday 14 November

1 Are you a patient or impatient person? When has Paul's admonition to the Thessalonians – 'be patient with everyone' (1 Thessalonians 5:14, NIV) – been a challenge for you? Why was it a challenge? What did this experience teach you about patience? What did it teach you about yourself?

2 When has an annoying or frustrating situation turned out to be a blessing and a reason for praising God? How did this experience affect the way you have handled other annoying or frustrating situations since?

3 Do you think the world would be a better place if we were more patient with one another? Why or why not?

4 What examples of patience do you see in scripture? What examples of impatience? Do you think being impatient is a sin? Is there ever a time when being impatient is appropriate?

5 What irritating situation are you dealing with today? For what in this situation can you praise God?

Wednesday 21 November

1 When was the last time you were out of your comfort zone? How does being out of your comfort zone make you feel? Should we as Christians always be comfortable?

2 If you were Peter, do you think you would have had the courage and trust to get out of the boat? Why or why not?

3 The 'Thought for the day' says, 'Before I can follow Jesus, I have to get out of the boat.' What 'boat' do you need to step out of today to follow Jesus? What challenges will this present? What opportunities?

4 Would you describe yourself as an adventurous and risk-taking person? Do you think you could be a better disciple were you to be more adventurous and risk-taking? When does being a true disciple require risk?

5 Can you think of a time when you faltered but Jesus was there to catch you? What effect did this experience have on you as his disciple? How did it change your attitude towards doing what Jesus calls us to do?

Wednesday 28 November

1 How often do you invite people to church? How many accept your invitation? Why do you think some people are reluctant to come to church when you invite them? What would you say to those who are reluctant?

2 The writer of today's meditation says, 'When we persevere in prayer and never give up, but continue to ask in prayer with faith, God will answer.' Is this always true? Does God ever refuse an answer to our prayers?

3 Have you ever prayed for something for a long time, only to have God answer your prayer years later? Why does it take God so long sometimes to answer our prayers? Why does he not answer all of them immediately?

4 The writer shows his friend concern and compassion during a difficult time. What role do you think this played in his friend's decision to come to church? What does this say about how we should behave towards those for whom we are praying?

5 Do you think God ever becomes annoyed with us when we ask for the same thing over and over and over? Why or why not?

Wednesday 5 December

1 When have you received a gift that probably wouldn't mean much to another person but was very meaningful to you? What was the gift? Who gave it to you? Why was it so special?

2 Can we ever give back to God all that he has given us? Why or why not? Use examples from your own life to illustrate your point. What does God want us to give in return for what we have been given?

3 When in your life have you struggled to give of your gifts? Why was it a struggle?

4 How does God expect us to both use and give of our gifts? When have you used your gifts to serve God in a surprising way? In what new ways could you use your gifts to serve God and others?

5 Name three ways that you will show your gratitude to God in the coming week by giving to others.

Wednesday 12 December

1 Are you someone who often compares your worth to others? Why is this sometimes easy and tempting to do? By what standards should we measure our worth?

2 The 'Thought for the day' says, 'When I measure my worth by God's standards, I am always enough.' What are God's standards of worth? How can we be sure that we are measuring our worth by his standards?

3 What would you say to someone who feels inadequate and useless? When have you felt like this? What helped you overcome these feelings and gain a greater sense of worth in God's kingdom?

4 Who are some 'lowly' people in scripture whom God used to accomplish great things? What do their stories teach us about what God sees in us and values in us? Which of these stories do you find most inspiring and encouraging?

5 For what purpose do you think you were designed? Why is it important that we let others know that they are valued and worthwhile in

God's eyes? Who in your life do you need to tell that they are valued and worthwhile in God's kingdom?

Wednesday 19 December

1 The writer of today's meditation says, 'I was confusing busyness with holiness, wants with needs and personal pride with ministry.' Say more about what you think she means by this statement. How do you relate to her experience? When have you done the same?

2 How often do you take time out of your busy schedule to be alone with God? Is having time alone with him easy for you or is it a challenge? Why is spending time alone with God important for all of us?

3 Why did Jesus need to spend time alone with God? In what ways do you think this helped him in his ministry? Do you think Jesus ever became as overwhelmed and tired as we sometimes become?

4 Have you ever 'hidden' behind your busyness in an attempt to ignore a problem? What happened? What did you learn? What would you say to someone doing the same thing today?

5 In the coming week, commit to spending 15 minutes each day alone with God. What busyness can you leave alone to make this happen? What will this time alone with God look like for you, and what do you hope to gain from it?

Wednesday 26 December

1 Have you ever felt 'limited' by the attitudes, judgements or opinions of other people? Speak about this experience. What did you do? What does scripture say about our own limitations and the limitations we place on others?

2 What do you think the writer means by, 'Our perception of the world can limit our understanding of the limitless possibilities Christ offers.' What does it mean for us that we have limitless possibilities in Christ?

3 Does God put any limitations on our ministry and what we can accomplish in the world? If so, what are they? Why would God put limitations on us?

4 In what ways would it change the church and the world were we all to believe that through Christ anything is possible?

5 What potential do you see in yourself to grow? What potential for growth do you see in others? How will you work to reach your full potential? In what ways can you help others reach their full potential?

Journal page

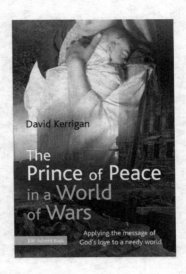

The biblical title 'The Prince of Peace' leaves us in no doubt that God's
purpose in Jesus Christ is to bring peace – universal peace, both with God
and with our neighbours. But have we really understood what this peace
might look like, especially in a world of wars and suffering? David Kerrigan
sees the coming of Jesus at Christmas as central to the divine plan to
bring peace to the world. Through reflection on biblical texts and mission
stories he locates God at the centre of our mission and encourages us to
restore the peace, joy and hope that come from accompanying Jesus.

The Prince of Peace in a World of Wars
Applying the message of God's love to a needy world
David Kerrigan
978 0 85746 570 2 £8.99
brfonline.org.uk

Few would doubt that we live in a wounded and broken world. But God has sent a Saviour, Jesus Christ, who calls us, in the beatitudes, to live an authentic, countercultural lifestyle. By being different we can make a difference, becoming the salt of the earth and the light of the world. Through living the beatitudes, we could make the world a better place. Will Donaldson explores and applies Jesus' beatitudes for today, exposing the value systems of the world and challenging us to live differently. As Christians, we can make a difference in the world through lives that reflect the values of the kingdom of heaven.

Living Differently to Make a Difference
The beatitudes and countercultural lifestyle
Will Donaldson
978 0 85746 671 6 £8.99
brfonline.org.uk

This inspirational book takes the reader through Advent to the celebration of Christmas through the eyes and beliefs of Celtic Christianity. Starting in November and reflecting on Jesus' coming at his birth as well as into our lives by the Holy Spirit and at the world's end, the author offers a unique approach to the season to help you gain a new sense of wonder in the birth of Jesus, the Saviour of the world.

Celtic Advent
40 days of devotions to Christmas
David Cole
978 0 85746 744 7 £8.99
brfonline.org.uk

From the author of *Postcards from Heaven* comes this unusual and beautiful gift. *Postcards of Hope* is a collection of original, beautiful watercolours by Ellie Hart, each with a short reflection aimed at helping the reader hear from God. For the tired and weary and those who want to have God breathe new life into their relationship with him.

Postcards of Hope
Words and pictures to breathe life into your heart
Ellie Hart
978 0 85746 648 8 £8.99
brfonline.org.uk

How to encourage Bible reading in your church

BRF has been helping individuals connect with the Bible for over 90 years. We want to support churches as they seek to encourage church members into regular Bible reading.

Order a Bible reading resources pack
This pack is designed to give your church the tools to publicise our Bible reading notes. It includes:

- Sample Bible reading notes for your congregation to try.
- Publicity resources, including a poster.
- A church magazine feature about Bible reading notes.

The pack is free, but we welcome a £5 donation to cover the cost of postage. If you require a pack to be sent outside the UK or require a specific number of sample Bible reading notes, please contact us for postage costs. More information about what the current pack contains is available on our website.

How to order and find out more
- Visit **biblereadingnotes.org.uk/for-churches**.
- Telephone BRF on +44 (0)1865 319700 Mon–Fri 9.15–17.30.
- Write to us at BRF, 15 The Chambers, Vineyard, Abingdon OX14 3FE.

Keep informed about our latest initiatives
We are continuing to develop resources to help churches encourage people into regular Bible reading, wherever they are on their journey. Join our email list at **biblereadingnotes.org.uk/helpingchurches** to stay informed about the latest initiatives that your church could benefit from.

Introduce a friend to our notes
We can send information about our notes and current prices for you to pass on. Please contact us.

Subscriptions

The Upper Room is published in January, May and September.

Individual subscriptions
The subscription rate for orders for 4 or fewer copies includes postage and packing:
The Upper Room annual individual subscription   £16.95

Group subscriptions
Orders for 5 copies or more, sent to ONE address, are post free:
The Upper Room annual group subscription   £13.50

Please do not send payment with order for a group subscription. We will send an invoice with your first order.

Please note that the annual billing period for group subscriptions runs from 1 May to 30 April.

Copies of the notes may also be obtained from Christian bookshops.

Single copies of *The Upper Room* cost £4.50.

Prices valid until 30 April 2019.

Giant print version
The Upper Room is available in giant print for the visually impaired, from:

Torch Trust for the Blind
Torch House
Torch Way
Northampton Road
Market Harborough   Tel: +44 (0)1858 438260
LE16 9HL   torchtrust.org

All our Bible reading notes can be ordered online by visiting biblereadingnotes.org.uk/subscriptions

☐ I would like to take out a subscription myself (complete your name and address details once)
☐ I would like to give a gift subscription (please provide both names and addresses)

Title .... First name/initials .... Surname ....

Address ....

.... Postcode ....

Telephone .... Email ....

Gift subscription name ....

Gift subscription address ....

.... Postcode ....

Gift message (20 words max. or include your own gift card):

....

....

Please send *The Upper Room* beginning with the January 2019 / May 2019 / September 2019 issue (*delete as appropriate*):

Annual individual subscription ☐ £16.95 Total enclosed £ ....

Method of payment

☐ Cheque (made payable to BRF) ☐ MasterCard / Visa

Card no. ☐☐☐☐ ☐☐☐☐ ☐☐☐☐ ☐☐☐☐

Valid from ☐M ☐M ☐Y ☐Y   Expires ☐M ☐M ☐Y ☐Y

Security code* ☐☐☐   *Last 3 digits on the reverse of the card
ESSENTIAL IN ORDER TO PROCESS THE PAYMENT

THE UPPER ROOM GROUP SUBSCRIPTION FORM

**All our Bible reading notes can be ordered online by visiting
biblereadingnotes.org.uk/subscriptions**

☐ Please send me .... copies of *The Upper Room* January 2019 / May 2019 /
September 2019 issue (*delete as appropriate*)

Title .... First name/initials .... Surname ....
Address ....
.... Postcode ....
Telephone .... Email ....

Please do not send payment with this order. We will send an invoice with your first order.

Christian bookshops: All good Christian bookshops stock BRF publications. For your
nearest stockist, please contact BRF.

Telephone: The BRF office is open Mon–Fri 9.15–17.30. To place your order, telephone
+44 (0)1865 319700.

Online: brf.org.uk

☐ Please send me a Bible reading resources pack to encourage Bible reading in
my church

Please return this form with the appropriate payment to:
BRF, 15 The Chambers, Vineyard, Abingdon OX14 3FE

To read our terms and find out about cancelling your order, please visit **brfonline.org.uk/terms**.

The Bible Reading Fellowship is a Registered Charity (233280)

UR0318

order

ne: **brfonline.org.uk**
phone: +44 (0)1865 319700
—Fri 9.15–17.30

Delivery times within the UK are normally
15 working days. Prices are correct at the time of
going to press but may change without prior notice.

le	Price	Qty	Total
e Prince of Peace in a World of Wars	£8.99		
ing Differently to Make a Difference	£8.99		
ltic Advent	£8.99		
stcards of Hope	£8.99		

POSTAGE AND PACKING CHARGES			
Order value	UK	Europe	Rest of world
Under £7.00	£2.00	£5.00	£7.00
£7.00–£29.99	£3.00	£9.00	£15.00
£30.00 and over	FREE	£9.00 + 15% of order value	£15.00 + 20% of order value

Total value of books	
Postage and packing	
Donation	
Total for this order	

ase complete in BLOCK CAPITALS

tle .... First name/initials .... Surname ....

ddress ....

.... Postcode ....

cc. No. .... Telephone ....

mail ....

ethod of payment

❏ Cheque (made payable to BRF)   ❏ MasterCard / Visa

ard no. ☐☐☐☐ ☐☐☐☐ ☐☐☐☐ ☐☐☐☐ ☐☐☐☐

alid from ☐M☐M ☐Y☐Y   Expires ☐M☐M ☐Y☐Y   Security code* ☐☐☐
Last 3 digits on the reverse of the card

ignature* .... Date .... / .... / ....
ESSENTIAL IN ORDER TO PROCESS YOUR ORDER

he Bible Reading Fellowship Gift Aid Declaration

giftaid it

lease treat as Gift Aid donations all qualifying gifts of money made
❏ today, ❏ in the past four years, ❏ and in the future **or** ❏ My donation does not qualify for Gift Aid.
am a UK taxpayer and understand that if I pay less Income Tax and/or Capital Gains Tax in the current tax
ear than the amount of Gift Aid claimed on all my donations, it is my responsibility to pay any difference.
lease notify BRF if you want to cancel this declaration, change your name or home address, or no longer
ay sufficient tax on your income and/or capital gains.

ase return this form to: BRF, 15 The Chambers, Vineyard, Abingdon OX14 3FE | **enquiries@brf.org.uk**
read our terms and find out about cancelling your order, please visit **brfonline.org.uk/terms**.

The Bible Reading Fellowship (BRF) is a Registered Charity (233280)

BRF

Transforming
lives and communities

Christian growth and understanding of the Bible

Resourcing individuals, groups and leaders in churches for their own
spiritual journey and for their ministry

Church outreach in the local community

Offering three programmes that churches are embracing
to great effect as they seek to engage
with their local communities
and transform lives

Teaching Christianity in primary schools

Working with children and teachers to explore Christianity creatively
and confidently

Children's and family ministry

Working with churches and families to explore Christianity creatively
and bring the Bible alive

Visit **brf.org.uk** for more information on BRF's work

brf.org.uk